# Sunday School That Really Excels

**Other Books on Sunday school by Steve R. Parr**
*Sunday School That Really Works*
*Sunday School That Really Responds*

# Sunday School That Really Excels

## Real Life Examples of Churches with Healthy Sunday Schools

### Steve R. Parr
EDITOR

**Kregel** *Ministry*

*Sunday School That Really Excels: Real Life Examples of Churches with Healthy Sunday Schools*

© 2013 Steve R. Parr

Published by Kregel Publications, a division of Kregel, Inc., P.O. Box 2607, Grand Rapids, MI 49501.

All Scripture quotations, unless otherwise indicated, are from the New King James Version. Copyright © 1982 by Thomas Nelson, Inc. Used by permission. All rights reserved.

Scripture quotations marked HCSB are from the Holman Christian Standard Bible®. Copyright © 1999, 2000, 2002, 2003 by Holman Bible Publishers. Used by permission.

ISBN 978-0-8254-4318-3

Printed in the United States of America
13 14 15 16 17 / 5 4 3 2 1

*To Dr. Billy Britt for his faithfulness
in leading Sunday Schools to excel
and for his personal devotion
and friendship*

# CONTENTS

# FOREWORD

ANY UNDERTAKING BY THE BODY of Christ for the cause of Christ should be done with *excellence*. Our Lord and Savior deserves the very best from his redeemed people. Therefore, the church of Jesus Christ ought to *excel*. This is especially true for Sunday school and for small groups. You see, small Bible study groups like Sunday school are the body of Christ on mission. Sunday school activates and mobilizes the army of God like nothing else. Think of it. Nothing engages God's people in the work of God on Earth like Sunday school. Sunday school is the layperson's ministry that can employ the spiritual giftedness of a larger part of a congregation more than any other ministry in the church.

Within each believer, God has placed seeds of *excellence*. This is so because the Holy Spirit dwells in every true child of God. Because God, in the person of the Holy Spirit, resides in us, we have *excellence* from within. Therefore, God himself has empowered us to *excel*. Sunday school is the greatest venue the church possesses which allows her members to express the *excellence* of God. The great apostle Paul taught this principle in Ephesians 3:9–11: "to make all see what is the fellowship of the mystery, which from the beginning of the ages has been hidden in God who created all things through Jesus Christ; to the intent that now the manifold wisdom of God might be made known by the church to the principalities and powers in the heavenly places, according to the eternal purpose which He accomplished in Christ Jesus our Lord."

Because God has endowed us to *excel*—because Sunday school is one of the greatest venues for disciples to excel—*Sunday School That Really Excels*, then, becomes such a valuable resource in helping us accomplish "the eternal purpose which He accomplished in Christ Jesus our Lord."

Steve Parr is a great champion and leader for Sunday school. This man knows his stuff, but he has also gathered some of the greatest Sunday school minds in North America, those who themselves have *excelled* in this work to provide wisdom and insights from their storied careers to aid church leaders. In addition, case studies have been provided for our edification. This book represents expertise from great Christian leaders and experiences from other churches, which form a powerful storehouse of usefulness for anyone wanting to use and grow their Sunday school.

Too many Sunday schools have wallowed in mediocrity for years. We have been satisfied to have "lukewarm" Sunday school ministries. We have been satisfied to allow this "Most Valuable Ministry" in the church to run on auto pilot. I am afraid we have fallen in love with our rhetoric about Sunday school more than *excelling* at Sunday school.

Jesus isn't the poster boy for status quo. He turned the religious system of his day on its proverbial head. Jesus was willing to turn Judaism upside down, so don't think for even a skinny minute that our religious institutions are safe. Are we raising believers in the cocoon of a domesticated Sunday school class and then wonder why they never get on mission with God? Being a soldier for Christ does not afford us the option of living a normal civilian life. When we get saved, we are placed smack-dab in the middle of a battleground, not a playground. Therefore, Sunday school should be a boot camp preparing soldiers for the spiritual battle, not a place for religious games. Our goal is not to provide a cozy cocoon for civilized faith to exist. Soldiers are trained to advance and take territory.

Two words that always go together—greatness and *excellence*. Great leadership is the pursuit of excellence. Without *excellence*, mission will not be accomplished. Sunday school leader, nothing tells your people what is important as that which you pursue with *excellence*. It's time to make a shift from just existing and move to *excelling*. Sunday school leader, if not you, who? If not now, when? If not this resource, what?

Come on now, Commanding Officer, let's rally the troops and charge enemy lines as we *excel* in the work and mission of Sunday school!

—Allan Taylor
Minister of Education
First Baptist Church
Woodstock, GA

# MEET THE AUTHORS

**STEVE R. PARR** is the author and compiler. He is the author of *Sunday School That Really Works* and *Sunday School That Really Responds*. He currently serves the Georgia Baptist Convention as the Vice-President of Staff Coordination and Development.

**KEN COLEY** is a professor and Director of Ed.D. Studies at the Southeastern Baptist Theological Seminary in Wake Forest, North Carolina.

**DAVID FRANCIS** serves as Director of Sunday School for Lifeway Christian Resources.

**LEROY GAINEY** is a professor of Educational Leadership at the Golden Gate Seminary in Mill Valley, California, and has served twenty-two years as pastor of Vacaville Baptist Church.

**SAM GALLOWAY** is a consultant to churches and state conventions in the North Central States for Lifeway Christian Resources.

**JOSH HUNT** is a pastor, author of numerous books including *You Can Double Your Class in Two Years or Less* and *Make Your Group Grow*. Josh is a national speaker and currently lives in Las Cruces, New Mexico.

**GARY JENNINGS** serves as the Network Specialist for Lifeway Christian Resources.

**BOB MAYFIELD** is the Sunday School/Small Group Specialist for the Baptist General Convention of Oklahoma.

**BEN PRITCHETT** is the Minister of Education for the First Baptist Church of Houston, Texas.

**TIM S. SMITH** is the Specialist for Sunday School and Small Groups of the Georgia Baptist Convention.

**ELMER TOWNS** is the cofounder of Liberty University in Lynchburg, Virginia, and serves as Dean of the School of Religion.

**ALLAN TAYLOR** is the Minister of Education at the First Baptist Church of Woodstock, Georgia.

**J.D. "SONNY" TUCKER** is the Executive Director of the Arkansas Baptist State Convention.

# ACKNOWLEDGMENTS

*SUNDAY SCHOOL THAT REALLY WORKS* was released in 2010. It caught fire and continues to be regarded as the leading "101" book to energize and revitalize a Sunday school ministry. *Sunday School That Really Responds* followed within two years and quickly became a high-demand resource that serves as the 911 for assisting church leaders in confronting common Sunday school challenges. I am so pleased that the series has now extended to include *Sunday School That Really Excels*. You will be encouraged as you take a journey across North America, going behind the scenes in real life churches that have thriving Sunday school ministries.

My life and ministry are the result of many influences throughout my lifetime. I served many years alongside a dear friend named Dr. Billy Britt. I have known him since I was a child and was privileged to serve with him on two different staffs for over fourteen years. We have done countless conferences together, strategized for ministry together, and coordinated training opportunities on many occasions. In recent years, we have served in different areas of our state and have been hindered from the frequent interactions to which I had become so accustomed. He is like a big brother to me and a valued partner in ministry. He is at a different stage of life now, and God continues to use him greatly. I am honored to be his friend and to dedicate this book to someone who has made such a difference in so many lives.

I can hardly believe the lineup of contributors that I was able to pull together to produce this book. It is a literal Who's Who in contemporary Sunday school leadership. I commend any book or any conference that you ever come across with their names: Allan Taylor, Josh Hunt, Elmer Towns, David Francis, Tim Smith, Leroy Gainey, Ken Coley, J.D. "Sonny" Tucker, Bob Mayfield, Ben Pritchett, Sam Galloway, and Gary Jennings.

I am thankful for the excellent staff at Kregel Publications. They have been a blessing to me, and God is using the staff to touch many lives through publishing excellent Christian books and resources. You are a blessing to leaders like me that desire to maximize their influence for the cause of Christ. I also want to say a special thanks to my good friend, Lori Swofford Palmer, for assisting with the editing and formatting of this project in preparation for the publishers.

Most of all, I am thankful to God for his blessings and provision. It is only by his grace and power that I can accomplish anything at all. It is ultimately to his glory that I present this book and myself.

—Steve R. Parr

# INTRODUCTION

David Francis

CAN YOUR SUNDAY SCHOOL STILL excel today? Really? I think by the time you finish reading the accounts in this book, you will join me in responding, "Absolutely! They really can—and do!"

One of the grand privileges I have as Director of Sunday school among Southern Baptists is to witness excellent Bible study ministries all across the country. I just enjoyed a little "slide show" in my mind of excellent Sunday school leaders and ministries I have witnessed firsthand. They are everywhere. They can be found in military communities like Lakewood, Washington, and Warner Robbins, Georgia. They are found in downtown areas like Tulsa, Oklahoma. You can find them in suburbs like Trussville, Alabama and Wheat Ridge, Colorado. You can find churches that actually have three separate Sunday school hours to accommodate all of the participants in places like Jackson, Tennessee.

They are found in college towns like Murray, Kentucky and Newark, Delaware, as well as in border towns like Athens, Alabama and McAllen, Texas. Midsized towns like Camden, Ohio and Madison, Mississippi. They are near the water in Lakeside, Texas as well as arid places like San Angelo, Texas and Casa Grande, Arizona. You will even find them amid the hectic pace of the District in Fredericksburg, Virginia and Upper Marlboro, Maryland or the rural pace of Princeton, Kentucky, growing where the population is booming in places like San Antonio, Texas and Fayetteville, Georgia, and in places where the population is stagnant like Roscommon, Michigan and Cross Lanes, West Virginia.

I didn't name the churches in these places. You can try to guess if you like. Central, Southside, Spotswood, Morningside, Glen Meadows, Faith, Deerfoot, Englewood, Parkhills, New Hope, Lindsay Lane, and a lot of Firsts. I absolutely fell in love with one church I visited this past year: First Baptist Winnsboro (Texas). If I had written a chapter about it, it might have been titled "Excelling in a small town where most of the staff is named David." Pastor David Rose, Minister of Education David Booth, student minister David Henry, and the other staff members, Scott and Jennifer Bowman, are all clearly committed to Sunday school. I led an all-adult Sunday school—about Sunday school, preached a message about the priority of reaching kids, and enjoyed lunch among some of the most enthusiastic folks I have ever been around. They got it! This is not an exceptional town. It is certainly not an exceptional building. It is a very typical and traditional church architecturally. The church has worked hard, however, to enhance its space for kids, doing much of the work with their own hands. It is seeing young families attend as a result. It works diligently at outreach. Some of its adult classes have moved to businesses off-campus to make room for growth. What I loved about this church is their commitment to have an excellent Sunday school whether all of the resources were present or not. After all, they did provide excellent training.

Seriously, what's the point of the example of FBC Winnsboro? They are not waiting. They are not waiting for the town to get bigger, the church to get prettier, the staff to get smarter, or the people to get more committed. They are excelling with what God has given them in the location He has placed them for the time He has granted them. They are committed to training their leaders, enlisting more of them, and motivating the members to embrace Sunday school as a missionary movement to reach their town for Jesus. Their attitude excels. Their hope excels. Their vision excels. Their Sunday school excels.

Maybe your church is more like FBC Winnsboro than it is one of the suburban megachurches you know of. Most are! In my denomination, more than ten thousand churches average less than fifty in Sunday school. Another ten thousand average less than one hundred. Only about three thousand average more than 250! The rest are in between. In the churches I serve, a church is above average at seventy-five to eighty in weekly attendance. What if? What if a lot of smaller churches decided to break out of double digits and exceed one hundred in attendance? What if a lot of midsize churches decided to break into the top ten percent by exceeding 250? You need not set your sights on megachurch status to excel in Sunday school. You just need to set them a little bit higher. If you will, the book you are about to read will help on your quest to excel.

What makes this book different is that it is not just a book of principles. It is a book of stories. Stories are powerful. These are real stories about real churches in real places with real leaders who face real circumstances and overcome real challenges. For what? To gather people—people with stories—together to learn, discuss, and apply God's story to their stories. If you've read any of my little books, you know I often repeat this principle: "No one's story is complete until it has intersected with God's story, which happens best in a community being enriched by the stories of others." I know of no better environment for that to happen than in a Sunday school that excels.

Another thing that sets this book apart is the storytellers—the men who have contributed the various chapters. They know Sunday schools. All are well traveled. Their experience is not limited to a few churches they have personally served—although each has served churches and led their Sunday schools to excel. They have been in lots of churches. They have seen all kinds of situations. Each could tell many more stories.

Leroy Gainey is a seminary professor, but he has also pastored and planted churches in the Northeast as well as the West, and he is the perfect person to tell the story of Sunday school in a multicultural environment. Ben Pritchett has grown Sunday schools everywhere he has served, and the story at his current church, Houston's First Baptist, is remarkable. Ken Coley is a master teacher, not just in the seminary classroom but in the Sunday school classroom too. Ken not only knows how to teach about teaching creatively but actually knows how to do it. I've experienced it myself.

The stories of hundreds of churches have been redirected by the ministry of "double your Sunday School" guru Josh Hunt, who is also living a personal story of leading a normal Sunday school to excel in the "middle of nowhere." Perhaps no one has exhorted Sunday schools to excellence through his speaking and writing than Elmer Towns. Of the many people who are known as "Mr. Sunday School" in the movement, he is perhaps most deserving. He is a lifelong student of, and champion for, the Sunday school movement.

Sam Galloway and Gary Jennings, who were the primary contributors to the stories in the chapters I coauthored with them, travel extensively across the Midwestern and Northeastern states as field representatives for LifeWay Christian Resources. Sam and Gary interact with dozens of church and denominational leaders every week. Either could tell a lot of other stories of Sunday schools that excel.

Perhaps no group spends more of each day thinking about, writing about, speaking about, and consulting about Sunday school than the folks who lead that work in Baptist state conventions. There are many great stories of excellent Sunday school work in Georgia. Steve Parr and Tim Smith are terrific partners in leading the movement in that state. They closely connect the work of evangelism with the mission of Sunday school, just as Sonny Tucker does so well in Arkansas. Sonny is also a great friend to the smaller church staffed with volunteers and is the perfect person to convey their stories. My buddy Bob

Mayfield, who leads the work of Sunday school in Oklahoma, shares my belief that the best days for the Sunday school movement—whatever it is called in local churches—are ahead of us, if churches will rediscover the basics.

Encouraging stories. Experienced storytellers. That's why this book is unique—and important. Like the previous two books in the series, you can read this book straight through, or you can skip to the stories that seem most applicable to your situation. One way a church leader might use this book is to read it privately and teach its concepts to others he or she leads. That's not how I would do it. I would recommend it be used the same way I suggest my little books be used. Provide your leaders a copy. Ask them to read a chapter. Then get together and talk about it. Everyone might not agree with everything in that chapter. You might not, either. That's okay. The main thing is to have a conversation. A conversation about what we do like. What we might do. To see our Sunday school excel!

So get started! Wherever you want to start. Just start somewhere. Thanks goes to Steve Parr for pulling these great stories together. Steve, myself, and the other contributors think you'll be blessed. And we'd love to hear your story! Maybe there could be another volume. What would you title your story? Our Sunday School excels.... It's your story to write. We all hope this book gives you the jump-start you need to "write" it.

# CHAPTER 1

# The State of Sunday School Today

*Steve R. Parr*

THE DRIVE FROM ATLANTA TO Nashville is pleasant and scenic. The drive is due north beginning on I-75, and expressway travel allows for uninterrupted progress except for the preferable breaks that the traveler chooses along the way. You will see the Georgia pines, get a panoramic view of Chattanooga, Tennessee, and climb Monteagle before pulling into the city of Nashville in less than four hours of travel. I'm on my way to interview one of the leading voices on the growth and health of churches from across North America.

Dr. Thom Rainer served for many years as the dean of the Billy Graham School of Evangelism at the Southern Baptist Theological Seminary in Louisville, Kentucky. He currently serves as the president of Lifeway Christian Resources located in Nashville. LifeWay is well known as a book publisher and curriculum developer for groups of all kinds, as well as for its Christian resources and its 165 Christian bookstores across America. However, Rainer's expertise for the issues at hand comes from years spent as a researcher and an author.

With nearly thirty books to his credit, Rainer has established himself as one of the most knowledgeable voices of this generation on what it is that makes churches effective. I enthusiastically recommend any of his books and am honored to be a personal friend. In the spirit of full disclosure, I will point out that Dr. Rainer was the project supervisor who had responsibility for guiding my doctoral project while serving in Louisville, Kentucky. I entered the program because I wanted to learn from the best, and I was not disappointed. I want you to begin this journey as we learn about Sunday schools that really excel by sitting down with us as I interview Dr. Thom Rainer about the state of Sunday school today.

I want to point out before the interview begins that we both use the word "Sunday school" descriptively with appreciation that many congregations utilize other designations. We both agree that a Sunday school consists of Bible study groups for all ages that ordinarily meet on Sunday mornings in conjunction with a worship experience either before or afterwards. With that being said, let's step into his office and get an expert's perspective on the state of Sunday school.

**Parr:** Dr. Rainer, you have written almost thirty books largely related to the health and growth of churches, and I know that your work is largely research based. Is there any particular theme that runs through your books as you look back on them as a whole?

**Rainer:** As I think back over all that I have written then, I would have to say the common theme is best summed up in a book I wrote called "High Expectations." The theme or idea of high expectations runs through a lot of my books.

**Parr:** What are you referring to when you say "high expectations?"

**Rainer:** It comes down to this: When we believe in what God can do through us, the result is that we expect more of ourselves. In turn, we tend to expect more of our congregation because we want to do all that we can to please God. As a result of expecting more of ourselves and of those we lead, we begin to see good things happen within the church itself. It is God working in us and through us that inspires us to go above and beyond seeking to do our best. I have written books addressing the programmatic elements of church life as well as the dynamics of the influences that help us to connect and reach the unchurched. I was not cognizant as I was writing, but it has become clear as I reflect back. My first book was published in 1989. From that point up until the present, I can now see that in most of my books that there is a theme that God expects much of us. The expectation is not that we would earn our salvation but a response to his grace. Out of gratitude we should expect much of ourselves, and we should understand that we have the resources we need through him.

**Parr:** Share with me about your leadership journey specifically as it relates to Sunday school through the years.

**Rainer:** For me the journey goes back to when I was a deacon and a layman at Golden Springs Baptist Church in Alabama and became very active in the Sunday school as an adult. The reason I am going that far back is because I grew up in another denomination, and Sunday school was not important in my earliest experiences. Although I attended church services, I was not involved in Sunday school from my childhood years all of the way through my young adult life.

**Parr:** I assume that must have changed at some point.

**Rainer:** Yes, it did. What happened is that once I got married, my wife and I made the decision to join Golden Springs Baptist Church, in Anniston, Alabama. It was my wife who encouraged us to find a Sunday school class. That was a new concept to me. Being the dutiful husband that I was, I got involved with a Sunday school class and my experience evolved from that point. If you fast-forward to the present,

I find it amazing that some of the relationships I developed in that group are still dear to my wife and me today. That's going back to 1979. As one example, I still have a relationship with a young man named Jim that I led to the Lord after which I was able to get him involved in our Sunday school class. I have to credit the ministry of the Sunday school in helping me engage with the total life of the church.

**Parr:** So you went from uninvolved to very involved, and it obviously became important in your spiritual walk. I believe I recall that you were called to pastor as a young adult. How did that experience affect your Sunday school journey?

**Rainer:** Ironically, I shifted back the other way at one point. Keep in mind that when I was called to vocational ministry, the ministry of Sunday school was very much a part of my experience and my vocabulary. I brought that passion to seminary with me and then went on to pastor four churches. But somewhere along the journey during my ministry as a pastor, two things were taking place. First of all, I became enamored with what I viewed as cutting-edge strategies that I perceived to be innovative. That caused me to begin to ignore and devalue Sunday school for a season during my early pastoral ministry. That is a fatal mistake for any church that desires to have a strong Sunday school ministry. I was in good company because many who became fascinated with the church growth movement made the same mistake.

**Parr:** I know you are an advocate of Sunday school today. What was it that caused you to go back to being a huge supporter of Sunday school as a strategy for churches?

**Rainer:** It happened as I began to do research as the backdrop of my writing endeavors. I went into my research experiences believing Sunday school had good things to offer, but as part of the church growth movement my focus was more on whatever was newest, latest, or greatest. Sunday school

does not fit the template when you are busy
and that is what I was doing. The Sunday sch
goes back to the late 1780s with Robert Rail
leads many to interpret it as irrelevant. In one sense, the
Sunday school goes even further back because small groups
have existed in one form or another throughout the centuries. Unfortunately, I abandoned Sunday school like so many
others because I was always enamored with the latest and
greatest. As I began to write about some of the cutting-edge
strategies, I didn't necessarily bash Sunday school—although
in my earliest books I wasn't very positive about it. But I have
always been committed to do objective research.

**Parr:** What did your research reveal?

**Rainer:** In the course of honest research, I found over and over
there is a high correlation between the health of a church
and the implementation of a strong Sunday school type of
ministry. I was surprised because of my preceding bias at
how often it was specifically Sunday school that was the
core strategy at work in the healthiest churches. The research consistently affirmed the relationship between an
open group ministry like Sunday school and the ability of a
church to assimilate new members.

**Parr:** Explain for those who will be reading what you mean
when you say an "open group."

**Rainer:** An open group is a Bible study group that meets
weekly and can be joined at any time throughout the
year without any prerequisites. In addition, the research
that I conducted consistently revealed that when nonbelievers connected to open groups such as Sunday school,
it dramatically increased the likelihood of that person
coming to faith in Jesus as Savior. My research caused me
to go through a paradigm shift back to strong support of
Sunday school as a strategy that, when done correctly, can
strengthen a church.

**Parr:** So you were actually a Sunday school doubter early in your pastoral ministry.

**Rainer:** I actually admitted following my research for my book *High Expectations* that I had made been making a mistake. I called it "Confessions of the Sunday School Skeptic," if I remember correctly. I admitted in writing that I was absolutely wrong. I believe the reason some church leaders struggle with the concept of the Sunday school is because they forget the purpose behind it. Sunday school, done correctly, enables your congregation to fulfill the Great Commission by integrating and balancing evangelism, discipleship, and ministry to members as well as the community. That has been my journey. I believe in Sunday school, and I think it is still relevant for churches today.

**Parr:** I know the name "Sunday school" emerged early on because it was established in its earliest form as a "school that met on Sunday" to battle illiteracy. Of course, Robert Raikes soon discovered that when you expose people to the Word of God, and the Bible served as the reading text, that God moves in hearts and lives. But when you consider that it is not school on Sunday and the fact that in some regions it is associated with ministry to children, there is a lot of discussion about the relevance of the name. Obviously, you support the strategy. What about the name itself? Should we change it?

**Rainer:** I actually fought for the name at one season of my ministry, but I don't do that anymore. Churches call it by all kinds of names. I realized it was a silly fight given the different names churches use such as Sunday morning bible study, Bible study group, open groups, fellowship groups, Bible Study Fellowship, connect groups, and on and on it goes. Many churches have already made that decision. The key is not what you call it so much as what you do with it. I believe in the strategy or the concept, but I am not married to the name as being critical to its success. There is no single answer. I know that's a cop-out answer. Let me give you an example. My son Sam served in his previous church in Sarasota, and I believe they called theirs "Life Groups." They ran into a problem. The Hispanic community that they were engaged with did not understand what Life Groups were, but they understood the name Sunday school, so they had to explain to the Hispanic community in southwest Florida that this is Sunday school. In addition, there are some regions where Sunday school is understood to be a ministry for children. I don't think the name "Sunday school" is intrinsically evil or intrinsically good. I think it has to be contextualized. It is more important to focus on the strategy than the name. The bottom line is that churches will be healthier if they involve their members in small groups like Sunday school as well as the larger gathering of a worship experience.

**Parr:** How would you characterize the state of Sunday school as a movement today?

**Rainer:** In many ways it is fledgling right now. But please do not misunderstand me on this point. I am not saying that it does not or cannot work or be effective. I am just acknowledging that fewer churches are focusing upon the concept of an open-group strategy than they did in years past. I believe that we are in a period of transition where worship has been the primary emphasis in an increasing number of churches. Another shift is underway now where the emphasis is shifting more toward missions and ministry as well as preaching. I'm not complaining because those are all good things. The challenge is that the emphasis on these is often at the expense of elevating the importance of connections to small groups such as Sunday school. My fear is, and I believe research will bear it out, that the devaluing the Sunday school or open groups may hasten the decline of involvement and attendance in Christian churches. You cannot build something while simultaneously minimizing or de-emphasizing it. I see it happening in individual congregations as well as on the national stage.

**Parr:** I was with a group of seminary students recently who were in master's level studies. I was disappointed when I asked what they had learned about leadership of the Sunday school ministry and the mechanics of leading it to be healthy and growing. Of the sixty students in the audience, I discovered that only one or two could recall anything tangible they had learned on the subject. Are you seeing any trends in higher Christian education that may be affecting the state of Sunday school?

**Rainer:** Steve, I am seeing the same thing. I know we both love our seminaries and Christian colleges, but I fear that fewer of them are talking about groups or Sunday school in the context of training future pastors on the skills needed to make it work effectively. Obviously, we are not talking about every seminary or every professor because so many do such a great job. We are talking about the trends of the day. Pastors are so critical to the health of Sunday school in a local church. If all of the emphasis is relegated to the Christian education track, then you are working around a key leader that needs the foundation himself. If the Christian-education wing of a school does not provide the tools for Sunday school leadership, then the erosion becomes even more challenging to address.

**Parr:** More and more churches are moving to small groups that meet during the week. I have not found it wise to dismantle the Sunday school in order to move to small groups in the churches where I serve, but that doesn't mean that I oppose small groups. It certainly makes sense for a church plant or a church lacking facilities to have weekday groups, and even churches that have Sunday schools can reach more by starting some groups during weekdays. Let me ask you. How has the small group movement affected Sunday school, in your opinion?

**Rainer:** Like you, I am a fan of all groups. I think that only good can happen when believers and unbelievers come together to study and talk about God's Word. It is certainly healthy for Christians to fellowship with one another and to work together to witness to nonbelievers. Therefore, whenever groups get together, I am a fan. I think the mistake that is being made is that leaders are creating a false dichotomy by asking which is better, Sunday school or small groups? It is not a competition. Suggesting that a church must choose one or the other, or that one is inherently superior is not beneficial to the body of Christ. But I do think that as a movement, the Sunday school has been hurt by the small group movement. Here is why. The elevation of weekday small groups as a strategy either through silence or overt disdain has diminished the value of Sunday school on some levels. I look back to where our denomination (Southern Baptists) were at a certain time, and a lot of people knocked Sunday school as a programmatic method. I would have to agree if a Sunday school ministry were an end instead of a means. Admittedly, some leaders have made it an end. However, when correctly applied, Sunday school is a means to engage your congregation in fulfillment of the Great Commission, and many congregations are still doing that successfully. We must be careful not to glorify the organization but to focus on and apply the intended purpose. The emerging anti-programmatic sentiment has dragged along with it Sunday school and closed groups as well, which is what many churches refer to as "Discipleship Training." I fear that we may have thrown the baby out with the bathwater, and the result is that there are fewer ongoing open groups in our churches today.

re the key factors that you find commonly at work
es that have strong Sunday schools?

first thing is that the pastor must be the primary advocate. I have always noticed that when the pastor fails to elevate the Sunday school as an integral part of the church life, it wanes. It is critical for the pastor to invest energy and time whether he is bivocational, single staff, or in a multi-staff situation. The pastor's influence is absolutely critical to the health of the Sunday school. It will crash if he fails to give support. Secondly, a strong core of lay leaders must be enlisted and equipped. Untrained leaders rarely, if ever, lead a Sunday school to be healthy and growing. The training takes on many forms in strong Sunday schools but is always there. Thirdly, the Sunday school must be elevated, or made a hero of the church. You accomplish that by giving examples through sermon illustrations, newsletters, and whatever means of communication a church has at its disposal to show how Sunday school is working within the church. Those are the starting points. You certainly have to follow that up by attending to organizational issues, facilities, creating new units, outreach, and so forth. Planning and participating in equipping opportunities is the source though which you address the other factors.

**Parr:** I know from reading your research that similarly to churches, some denominations have stronger Sunday school ministries than others. You do not limit your research to Southern Baptist churches. What makes the difference on that macro level, do you suppose?

**Rainer:** It may sound redundant but once again it comes down to leadership. Leadership is the key no matter the denomination and no matter the region. It is stronger where the denominational leaders support it and weaker when the denominational leaders devalue it whether inadvertently or by intent. I have noted that the theology of the denomination also bears great influence. I have found that the less conservative-leaning denominations value Sunday school less because they value the Bible less. God's word is the anchor of a healthy Sunday school. It is not enough to come together, but the body must be connected through the study of God's word as well as fellowship. Denominations certainly differ, and where the Bible is not valued, the need for groups like Sunday school lack value. I am glad to report, however, that some denominations are beginning to embrace Sunday school, and I have no doubt they will be strengthened in the long run.

**Parr:** What would you say are the key changes that have taken place in the Sunday school movement over the last generation?

**Rainer:** We have already addressed a couple of those. The name "Sunday school" is obviously being used less frequently. Secondly, there has been a shift towards more of an emphasis on the worship experience, and as I said earlier an emerging shift towards missions and ministries. A third trend that we have not discussed would be what is occurring in relationship to Bible study curriculum. We are seeing unevenness and inconsistency in curriculum. In the past, a pastor would not only have confidence that his sermon or sermon series was being approached strategically but also that the education ministries were using curriculum strategically. An inconsistency has emerged where one class may be studying a book, another class may have LifeWay or a denominationally driven curriculum, while yet another group has material from a completely different publisher. Still another group may just say "we are going to study the Bible" and not have any curriculum at all. I cannot imagine a pastor not having a plan for his preaching, but I find it amazing how many are so unorganized or non-strategic about the content being utilized in the Bible study groups. I certainly have affection for what my organization provides. But, at this point, I share this trend which is a growing concern without regard to the excellent materials we provide and fear that the "teach whatever you want" approach is detrimental to a healthy strategy in a local church.

**Parr:** What adjustments or adaptations do you think need to be made for Sunday schools in the current culture?

**Rainer:** We do not need to be afraid to call it something else. I think I have beat that horse till it's dead—not to be hung up on the name. Churches need to be innovative with the space that is available. I find when the Sunday school meets on the campus of the church that there is a greater likelihood of involvement of the members, and I can see many reasons why that would be the case. However, in many of our churches today, space is not available. Most church plants face this problem, and so you have to look to alternatives other than the campus itself. A willingness to be flexible about location and time is important. I have yet to find a better time than connecting the small group experience to the worship service primarily because of convenience. That does not mean that other alternatives should not be considered or will not work. I also want to emphasize again that you cannot take for granted what is being taught in your groups. You need to develop a strategic plan for content delivery in your Sunday School ministry to ensure the content is biblical, consistent with your church's theological convictions, and leads the group to action or application.

**Parr:** Let me ask you one more question, Dr. Rainer. How do you see evangelism and Sunday school connected?

**Rainer:** Well, of course, there are so many ways, where do I begin? It all begins with relationships. It is amazing how you bond with people that you meet with to study God's word on a regular basis. Those relationships enable you to serve together in reaching out to your friends and neighbors. I want to share something else. The older I get, Steve, the more I realize how powerful the word of God is. I wish I had realized it more when I was young. Robert Raikes tapped into it when he began Sunday school as a way to teach children to read. They used the Bible as their textbooks, and as a result of their reading scripture, the Holy Spirit worked through them with hundreds coming to faith in Jesus Christ. Is there a better way to introduce someone to Jesus than studying God's Word with them? That is the nature of an open group and ultimately the aim of Sunday school when correctly implemented. Relationships are built between believers and then between believers and members of the community. They can be brought in to visit or join at any point, and the group should be working together to bring unbelieving friends. Sunday school is intended to be evangelistic, and leaders who desire to have a healthy Sunday school will emphasize this aspect. Sunday schools can flourish if we are purposeful in leading them to be evangelistic.

**Parr:** Dr. Rainer, I could not agree more. I want to tell you how much I appreciate your friendship and your leadership among evangelical churches. I appreciate your helping our readers to think through some of the challenges we are facing in our Sunday schools. You are definitely to be commended for your work in encouraging and equipping leaders to develop Sunday schools that really excel!

## CHAPTER 2

# Excels in the Middle of Nowhere

## *Josh Hunt*

IF I WERE ASKED TO provide an alternate name for this chapter, it would be *The Normal Church*. The message of the chapter is simple: You can grow a church and still be normal. Imagine walking into your average Christian bookstore today. Find the section of books for pastors. Read the top twenty best-selling books for pastors. Now, answer this question: would you have the impression that you can grow a church and be normal? Would you have the idea you can grow a church using Sunday school? Would you have the idea that Sunday school is a vital way of growing a church today?

Read one book, and you would get the idea you have to be missional to grow a church today. Another one says you need to be seeker-driven. Yet another says you must be purpose-driven. Some experts say you must be innovative. Others suggest that house churches are the wave of the future. Still others say the opposite; you need a mega church to reach people today.

I remember reading *Simple Church* a few years back. (I love the book!) I was a member of First Baptist Las Cruces at the time, and they were having their annual Living Christmas Tree presentation. I don't have a lot of musical talent, but I do have skill in PowerPoint presentations, so I volunteered to help where I could. My job was to click the mouse about five times over the course of the two-hour presentation. With a lot of down time, I brought a book to read between mouse clicks.

Reading *Simple Church* while helping with the Living Christmas Tree was a study in contrasts. The Living Christmas Tree is anything but simple. Multiple choirs: adult choir, youth choir, senior adult choir, children's choirs, hand bells, ensembles, quartets, solos, orchestra, and a live baby Jesus. The lights would rival a Las Vegas-style show, with swishes and swipes and fades and blinks and color coordination all pulsing to the sound of the music. At the end of the show, they actually have stuff blow up. Who doesn't like a show where stuff blows up? Simple Church, that's who. I am reading about the glory of simplicity while in the midst of an incredibly complex presentation. I know this one hundred-year-old church will never be really simple. Can an un-simple church grow?

I believe that reading these types of books can potentially give us a distorted view of reality. It is like watching television, and all of the actors are beautiful and handsome. Have you ever noticed that the people on television don't look like the people at Walmart? Have you ever noticed that the churches you read about in church growth books don't sound like any church you have ever been to?

David Francis did some additional research about the simple churches. I was shocked by what he found:

> David Francis conducted a secondary project around the 400 Southern Baptist churches identified as "vibrant" to determine what kind of small group structure the churches operated. Gathering information from church websites and phone calls, he was able to gather information on 376 (94%) of the "vibrant" churches. Eighty-seven and a half percent (87.5%) of those

churches operated Sunday school—or a functionally comparable on-campus program scheduled adjacent to the primary worship service. Twelve and a half percent (12.5%) operated small groups, with the groups meeting primarily off-campus at times other than Sunday morning. Fifty-three percent (53%) of the vibrant churches used only the words "Sunday school" to describe the program, while 26% used terms like Bible Study, Bible Fellowships, LIFE Groups or other terms, and 8% used Sunday school together with another term.[1]

It turns out, these simple churches are more normal than we thought. Allow me to introduce you to Vansickle Baptist Church. They are an example of such a church.

Vansickle Baptist is a normal church. It is not innovative. Not seeker-driven. Not truly purpose-driven. Not simple. Yet, for twenty-one consecutive years they have grown. They grew in spite of the fact they didn't have the advantages that some churches have:

- **Location**. Vansickle is out in the middle of nowhere. I am not sure Tiger Woods could hit a man-made structure from any place on their property.
- **Facilities.** Their pastor told me that when he arrived there was actually a hole in the roof and you could see up into the attic.
- **Resources.** The first month the pastor came, there were eighteen people present—and five of them belonged to his own family.
- **Education.** Their pastor had no formal Bible training when he was called to serve. He later got a degree from D.

1.   Eric Geiger and David Francis, "Sunday School in a Simple Church," *LifeWay:* http://www.lifeway.com/lwc/files/lwcF_Sunday_School_in_a_Simple_Church.pdf. (April 25, 2013)

Edwin Johnson Bible School. D. Edwin Johnson is a fine enough school, but there is nothing about that training that explains twenty-one consecutive years of growth.

Allow me to introduce you to Pastor Roger Ratliff of Vansickle Baptist Church in Greenville, Texas.

- **Business background.** Roger worked for thirteen years as a manager of a photography company.
- **Sales background.** The photography company was bought out, and the new owners eliminated the seven top-paid employees at the firm. At the time, Roger felt it was the worst day of his life. In retrospect, it was a Romans 8:28 moment: one of the many things that God worked together for good.
- **Polio.** Roger was in and out of hospitals for months as a child. This may seem like an odd thing to include in a list of things God used to prepare Roger to be a church growth pastor. However, this experience drove an idea deep into Roger's soul: No one should have to go through this alone.

So, how did they do it? How were they able to see twenty-one consecutive years of growth? I put that question directly to Roger and his wife, and I got roughly the same answer from each: Roger is a hands-on pastor. He cares and shows it by his actions. If you are in the hospital, he is there. If your dog dies, he calls. If you have a birthday, he calls. If you are six years old, and you have a birthday, he calls. His door is always open. Members have his cell phone number. They can and do call him when they need him. People come to Vansickle because they are loved. Love is their secret church growth strategy.

Lyle Schaller talks about this strategy in *44 Ways to Increase Your Church Attendance*:

> While it is an expensive course of action in terms of time, energy, and frustration when people are not at home, the most

effective single approach to increasing church attendance in, perhaps, seven out of ten of all Protestant churches is for the minister to call in every home at least twice a year. In the 1950s that would have been at the top of this list.[2]

## DO OLD FASHIONED METHODS STILL WORK?

That last line might get your attention. You might be thinking, "Yeah, back in the '50s, but what about today?" Surely methods that worked in the '50s will not work anymore. There seems to be a widespread perception that the things that used to work don't work anymore.

I read a post on Facebook recently that illustrates this point. It said something like, "Fifty-three percent of people surveyed said they would not be open to a stranger telling them about their faith in God." There is a tendency to read something like that and think, "I guess old-fashioned witnessing doesn't work anymore."

My response: "Forty-seven percent are open to a stranger telling them about their faith in God."

I have a pastor friend in El Paso, Texas that doubled his church twice in six years—going from about 125 to more than five hundred. I asked him how he did it. I asked him specifically about his music. I asked about music because that seems to be a point of tension in a lot of churches I visit. "Bill, do you have a hot band?" A lot of church growth books and seminars say you have to have a hot band to reach people today.

"Hot band? No, we don't have a hot band. Our music is completely traditional." There is language you don't hear too much anymore. Completely traditional. Most people say their music is blended. At Vansickle, the music is blended. (Some say that blended music is music that keeps everyone equally unhappy, but this is a book on Sunday school, not music.)

---

2.  Lyle E. Schaller, *44 Ways to Increase Church Attendance* (Nashville, TN: Abingdon Press, 1988), 38.

"Completely traditional?" I wanted to make sure I had heard Bill correctly.

"Yes, in fact, it is bad traditional."

"What do you mean by bad traditional?"

"The piano is out of tune. The person playing doesn't play very well. The songs they sing are old but not the great old hymns of the faith. They are songs I would rather never hear again."

"How did you double a church twice in six years with music that isn't any better than that?"

Here is what Bill said he did: first day of work he shows up, gets a cup of coffee, and reads his Bible. Then he is out the door to knock on doors. He walks east from the church.

Door #1 is not home.

Door #2 is not home.

Door #3 is not home.

Door #4 is not interested.

Door #5 is not home.

Door #6 is not home.

Door #7 is nice but they go to another church. . .

At Door #50, Bill knocks on the door and introduces himself as the new pastor from the church down the street. He asks if there is anything he can pray for them about. The lady bursts into tears. "Yes. My mother is in the hospital. She is having surgery tomorrow. I am scared. Can you pray for her?" They pray. He volunteers to go visit her at the hospital. One thing leads to another, and the whole family comes to faith in the Lord Jesus Christ.

Day #2. Bill gets to work, pours a cup of coffee, and reads his Bible. Thirty minutes later he is out the door. This day he walks west. Bill does this every day, for four hours a day. Soon he starts reaching a few people. He develops some relationships in the church. He invites people to join him. The church grows. Income increases. He hires staff. He tells them if they come to work for him, they will be joining him for four hours a day of knocking on doors. Five years later, the church has doubled twice.

Here is the lesson. A lot of people who tell you things don't work anymore are wrong. The only reason they don't work is that we don't work them. I am not sure that bus ministry ever really stopped working. We just got tired and sold the buses.

Visitation is a method that has been around a long time. Does it still work? I researched this in preparation for my book *Make Your Group Grow*. Here is what I found: With classes that were *not involved in visitation*, twenty-nine percent were growing, and three percent reported that they were growing rapidly.

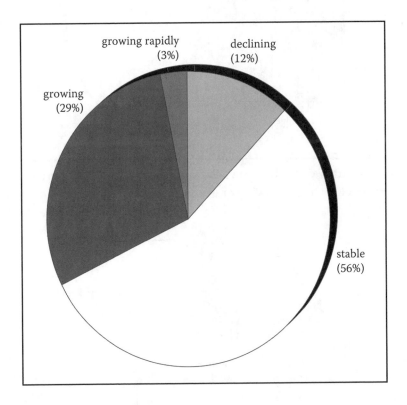

Groups that were involved in visitation were nearly twice as likely to grow—fifty-one percent growing and six percent growing rapidly.

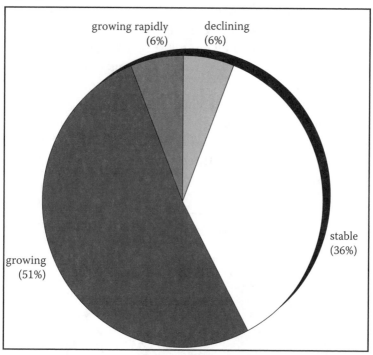

Churches involved in visitation were seventy-eight percent more likely to be growing or growing rapidly:

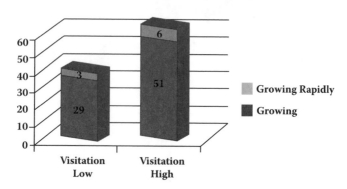

For years at Vansickle, they engaged in home visitation every Tuesday night. They did faith Evangelism for seven years. Is visitation the only way to grow a church? No. But it is one way, and it still works if you work it.

Ed Stetzer, Warren Bird, and Elmer Towns wrote a book on innovative churches. They researched some interesting models: house churches, recovery churches, multisite churches, and so forth. Here is the most brilliant line in the book: "We three authors have a strong bias that it takes all kinds of churches to reach all kinds of people."[3] I think Rick Warren said a similar thing in *The Purpose Driven Church*.

When radio came along, it didn't replace newspapers. When television emerged, people didn't stop listening to the radio. Now we get content on the Internet, but a lot of people still read the newspaper, listen to radio, and watch television. The new thing adds another option. It doesn't necessarily replace the old. We have new churches that do new things. Good for them. But God can use established churches too.

Vansickle has used pastoral care as a primary driver of their growth. It is an old-fashioned way, but it still works if you are willing to work it. But, there is one problem.

## WHAT GOT YOU HERE MAY NOT GET YOU THERE

Vansickle enjoyed twenty-one consecutive years of growth. But in recent years, they hit a bump. That is not surprising. The surprising thing is they were able to maintain growth through multiple growth barriers for twenty-one straight years. Big churches are not just bigger versions of smaller churches. They are different. People come to a church of five hundred

---

3.   Elmer L. Towns, Ed Stetzer, and Warren Bird, *11 Innovations in the Local Church: How Today's Leaders Can Learn, Discern and Move into the Future* (Ventura, CA: Regal Books, 2007), 19.

for a completely different reason than they might come to a church of fifty.

There are two big differences between a small church and a big one. In a small church, the pastor cares for everyone. In the words of Lyle Schaller, the pastor is a shepherd. He personally cares for the sheep. In a larger church, he is more like a rancher. He makes sure the sheep are cared for, but he doesn't do it all himself.

Leith Anderson tells the story of a conversation he had with a lady at the ticket counter at the airport. She invited him to attend her church that weekend. Leith was impressed and asked her what church she attended. "Wooddale Community Church," was her reply. Wooddale is the church Leith pastors. He is her pastor, and she didn't recognize him. She attended the Saturday night service that has another preaching pastor. Leith is the consummate rancher.[4]

For a church to grow large, the pastor has to become a pastor of pastors, a leader of leaders. The second difference between a big church and a small one is that in a small church, everyone knows each other. A big church will include overlapping groups that don't know each other. To become a big church, you have to be willing to worship with people you don't know. Often people think this is a function of the number of services, but it is more a function of size. I read something years ago that said they did a survey asking church members, "How many people in this church do you know?" In big churches and small, everyone knew about 150.

It turns out there is a reason for this:

British anthropologist Robin Dunbar did extensive investigation on this topic. He measured the neocortex of primates

---

4. Kevin E. Martin, *Myth of the 200 Barrier: How to Lead Through Transitional Growth* (Nashville, TN: Abingdon Press, 2005), 57.

and their typical group size. You may remember that the human brain is the largest of all primates. Dunbar found a direct relationship between brain size and the social size of groups. He set the human number at just over 147. Dunbar then studied 21 tribal peoples worldwide to test his number. What he discovered was remarkable. The average size of a tribal group was just over 148! This led Dunbar to formulate the Rule of 150. Briefly, this rule states that at 150, the number of relationships among people becomes so complex that the group must either divide or face social disintegration.[5]

I remember a stark example of this when I was on church staff. Our church grew from one service and one Sunday school to four services and four Sunday schools. We had a rotating deacon system where a certain number of deacons rotated on and off every year. They were elected by popular vote. I will never forget one deacons' meeting—the first of a year when new deacons had been elected. Two deacons—both elected by popular vote of the congregation—walked across the room, shook hands, and introduced themselves to each other. One was an active member of the Saturday night congregation while another was active in the 9:45 a.m. Sunday morning congregation. The two had never met. For a church to grow large, you have to be willing to worship with people you do not know.

Vansickle is addressing these issues and is in the early stages of starting to grow again. The have added staff. They have centralized the administration in an elder system. They have started new groups.

But, these are small church to large church changes. They are still a normal church. And, they are a shining example of the fact that normal churches can grow. We applaud what God is doing in new churches, innovative churches, house churches,

---

5.  Ibid, 40.

mega churches, seeker churches, purpose-driven churches, missional churches, and whatever is next churches. We also applaud what God is doing in normal churches. Whatever your hand finds to do, do it with all of your heart. God is at work and can work in your church even in the middle of nowhere.

# CHAPTER 3

# Excels in a Rural Area

## *Tim S. Smith*

CAN A SUNDAY SCHOOL MINISTRY thrive out in a rural community? The US Census Bureau, the USDA's Economic Research Services, and the US Office of Management and Budget all agree that a rural area is defined as having no city or town with a population of more than fifty thousand. They go further in stating that the rural area needs to be no less than 999 square miles or a population density of no greater than one person per square mile. A great example of a church that is excelling in a rural community is the Corinth Baptist Church in Haralson County, Georgia. A twenty-minute drive allows people in four counties to attend the church, and the total population within that zone is less than 48,000.

A closer inspection of the community living within a three-mile circle of the church provides an even better understanding of this particular mission field. The total population is only 2,983, and the growth in population has recently started to decline following twenty years of increase. The community surrounding the church is primarily Anglo and consists of an aging population. The traditional family is still very strong in the community, but there are an increasing number of single mothers. Seventy-five percent of the households are below the national level in average household income.

Some experts might propose that a church has no chance of experiencing growth under these circumstances. Don't say that, however, to the members of Corinth Baptist Church. John Lemmings said he knew his church was in a rural area when he was called as pastor because they are "a long distance from any city." He said it takes "over thirty minutes to drive to any store." He also stated "farming was very prominent in the community. Between forty and fifty percent of the families living within three miles of the church are either full-time or part-time farmers." The largest employer in the area is the Haralson County School System, but some drive well over an hour into the metro Atlanta area for work.

## CHALLENGES FOR THE RURAL CHURCH

All churches face difficulties, but the challenges for a rural church are unique. Let's consider four of the key challenges faced by rural congregations. The first challenge is the mindset of the members. The inherent limitations lead many to conclude that they are unable to accomplish anything significant in their own community much less beyond. Secondly, the members have to commute a great distance in order to participate in services, and this can limit the number of times during the week they are able to gather at the church.

Thirdly, many small, rural churches have an established power structure dominated by either one person or one family as the head. If this person or group is negative, it can greatly hinder the church's progress. Finally, and most importantly, the role of the pastor is commonly viewed as that of a preacher or chaplain and not as a leader. They are accustomed to the pastor doing the ministry, and the members providing the leadership and oversight of the congregation.

## THE LITTLE CHURCH THAT COULD

Corinth Baptist Church is 150 years old, and many of the present church families have historic ties with the founding members. The congregation has had a steady stream of pastors through the years, as well as church conflicts. Sixteen pastors have served in the past forty years with the average pastorate staying only two and a half years. During the last interim period following the loss of a pastor, the members realized that something needed to change and became desperate. In their words, "If God didn't do something, this place was going to shut down."

John Lemmings was most recently called as the new pastor and has been at this church for three years. During that time, God has done some very exciting things, and the church is alive and well. The resident church membership has increased from 154 to 438. Almost 120 new believers have been baptized in the past three years compared to less than fifty in the previous decade. While the worship attendance has doubled, the Sunday school enrollment has increased from fifty-eight to 356, and the average attendance in Sunday school has grown from forty-six to 187.

## A CHANGE IN MIND-SET

How is this congregation different from any other typical rural/small church? It begins with the mind-set of the members. They truly trust and expect God to do something great in their lives, their church, and their community. The attitude of the members is that their church can do something great for God not only in their community but also around the world. They do not allow the size of the church to be a limitation but rather an opportunity for God to work and get glory through their church. The congregation is blessed with godly leaders that desire to make a difference with the first priority to seek God's direction. As one deacon said, "We don't want to mess up what God is doing, or get in his way."

Another factor that distinguishes Corinth from many other small/rural churches is that the members are purposeful in embracing new members and accepting growth. They are very receptive to newcomers, whereas in many similar churches the established members resist and resent the addition of new members. The growth in numbers is present, but it should be noted that they are also seeking to grow spiritually as well as numerically. The spirit of the church is healthy because as one member stated, "We are not fussing and fighting." Though they may have been viewed by the community as a troubled church in years past, they are now known in the community as a loving group of people who really do care.

## THE STRATEGY THAT LED A RURAL CHURCH TO EXCEL

God is obviously blessing Corinth Church, and it is essential to remember that God wants to do a great work in all congregations. His Spirit and power is not limited by the size of a congregation. What are they doing that has allowed them to excel while so many others are experiencing decline?

First, they have a clearly defined mission and process. In every room, in every hallway, in every publication, and in every gathering the purpose of Corinth Baptist Church is communicated. It is "WIN every person, GROW every heart, and SEND every body." The biblical foundation for their mission is the Great Commission found in Matthew 28:19–20, "Go, therefore, and make disciples of all nations, baptizing them in the name of the Father and of the Son and of the Holy Spirit, teaching them to observe everything I have commanded you. And remember, I am with you always, to the end of the age" (HCSB). They are purposefully seeking every available opportunity to win every available person to Jesus Christ while using every available means. Every Sunday school class, each of the ministries, and all activities are viewed as opportunities to bring people to faith in Jesus Christ. They have opted to eliminate ministries if they hinder or fail to focus on reaching out to the community. The outward focus is critical, and it can be accomplished without neglecting the needs of the members.

Reaching out to the lost is important, but growing every heart is integral to the process as well. The church is also committed to helping believers to mature into devoted followers of Jesus Christ. They take very seriously 2 Peter 3:18, "But grow in the grace and knowledge of our Lord and Savior Jesus Christ. To Him be the glory both now and to the day of eternity. Amen" (HCSB). The members are encouraged to be active in personal Bible study and prayer every day. They are involved in small groups on a weekly basis, and corporate worship is also used as a teaching time through the preaching ministry of Pastor John.

The process does not end with bringing people to faith and aiding in their spiritual development through the study of God's Word. Serving Christ and sending leaders to engage in missions locally and globally are also given specific attention. Corinth is becoming a congregation similar to an Acts 1:8 church. "But you will receive power when the Holy Spirit has come on you, and you will be My witnesses in Jerusalem, in all Judea and Samaria, and to the ends of the earth" (HCSB). The congregation has developed ministries that are touching their local communities including a food pantry and a clothing closet for those in need locally. Mission trips are now a regular part of the church experience and mission's offerings have doubled in the past three years. The focus on the mission is communicated, and the process of evangelism, discipleship, and missions is highlighted continually. Mind-sets and attitudes have begun acclimating to the new focus.

The second element that is helping this church to excel is their commitment to Sunday school as their foundational strategy. Pastor John stated, "Sunday school has been the key ministry that has made a difference." Sunday school has become a priority ministry because it is the way the church organizes to accomplish the Great Commission. Every class is involved and organized to "WIN every person, GROW every heart, and SEND every body." It is through the groups that the mission is accomplished. The mission statement is the fuel, and the Sunday school is the vehicle. One teacher said, "We tried to grow the church through preaching and worship but it did not work."

Making Sunday school a priority will not eliminate every hindrance to growth. The following two issues will not cause or bring health and growth by themselves but can serve as barriers. The first hindrance that many small churches face when they experience growth is lack of meeting space. Growth may not be deterred but will ultimately be limited if worship and parking capacity is expanded while Bible study space is not likewise increased. Education space that is filled beyond capacity can severely limit future growth possibilities. Planning for space needs to include designs for growth in Sunday school as well as meeting immediate needs. A church can grow beyond capacity, but the climb gets steeper as the space gets more overcrowded.

Another hindrance faced by many small congregations is the quality of music provided in the worship service. This is a great challenge for many small/rural congregations. The style of the music is not nearly as critical as the quality that is provided. The church that fails to attend to resolving the issue of quality will likewise be limited rather than deterred in most circumstances. One of the benefits of reaching out to the community and experiencing growth is the likelihood that talent will come with the increase. Be mindful that quality is not perfection or professionalism, but seeking to do your best with the resources at hand. Technology can serve as an aid to provide tremendous enhancements to the music experience that would not have been available to previous generations.

The third element that has served Corinth in becoming an excelling church is the leadership of Pastor John Lemmings. He is a Sunday school pastor in every sense of the title. Pastor John has made the commitment to be the leader of the Corinth Baptist Church. He understands that he is not the boss but rather the example serving as the congregation's coach. When he first started at Corinth, he taught a class on Sunday mornings. That fact may not appear significant or unique at first glance. What is unusual is that Pastor John taught the fourth- and fifth-grade Sunday school class. He recognized early on the need to improve the ministry to children if the church was going to reach young families. The church had one class for elementary-age students, and no one to teach a new class. He stepped into the gap, and led it himself. Later he enlisted the new leaders for the class and now teaches a pastors' class on Sunday mornings.

John also leads the equipping meetings for Sunday school teachers at least once each quarter. The leaders meet during the week and have a meal with child care. Eighty percent of the leaders are in attendance at an average training session. He provides quality training that assists the teachers in accomplishing their leadership task. His goal is to equip the teachers to be more effective in their leadership, and therefore, makes each meeting primarily a time of instruction rather than a meeting for announcements and administration. Equipping the saints to lead their ministries is not only biblical, but also a tangible way that a pastor in a small congregation can generate momentum. While relationships are enhanced through this time together, the skills and the spiritual development of the leaders is promoted through the pastor's leadership.

John has always been personally evangelistic, sharing his faith and seeking to bring them into a relationship with Jesus. As a pastor, he is purposeful in leading his congregation to be evangelistic. He provides training for the members in how to share the gospel and leads them to practice sharing their faith. When a new believer makes their commitment public on a Sunday morning, the person that shared with them is also asked to stand with them. John also uses his sermons to provide ideas for classes and members to be evangelistic. In a recent sermon, he mentioned the idea of simply helping a senior adult at the grocery store load their groceries into the car. He later heard that the middle school girls Sunday school class had taken that idea and begun to apply it. A group of girls went to the local grocery store and did what the pastor had suggested. It made an impact not only on those that were assisted but also the store manager as well.

Pastor John also takes the lead in enlisting new leaders and creating new classes. In three years, the church has grown from eight Sunday school classes to eighteen classes. The ten new classes and all the leaders to staff those groups were personally enlisted and trained by the pastor. More leaders and more groups will ordinarily reach more people.

## PASTOR SAYS

There is no such thing as a wrong-sized church. Being a leader or a member of a small congregation is more common than being in a larger church. The mandate for the church is the same whether small or larger, whether urban, suburban, or rural. The mandate is the Great Commission. The error often made is not the size of the congregation but the failure to attend to the Great Commission.

A small rural church can excel, and Corinth is proof of that. Your church can be healthy and grow even when small or located out in the country, because the God you serve has no limitations. When your location, church size, or history appear to be working against you, the God that you serve is working for you. God is doing something great at Corinth, and the glory goes to him. He is also to be glorified because the people at Corinth have made a commitment and plan to keep moving in a direction consistent with the teaching of his Word. He is also to be glorified through the ministry of the pastor who has exceeded the average tenure of recent decades and is committed to lead the congregation for a long period of time.

In preparation for this chapter, Pastor John was asked this question; "If you were having a cup of coffee with a pastor from a small, rural church, and he asked what do I need to do, how would you respond?" He replied:

1. Persistent Prayer
2. Passionate Leadership
3. Purposeful Sunday School
4. Powerful Evangelism
5. Prominent Multiplication

That is sound advice. May God bless small, rural churches as they make a difference, like Corinth Baptist Church in Georgia!

# CHAPTER 4

# Excels in Revitalizing an Established Ministry

## Ben Pritchett

CAN A CHURCH, ESPECIALLY A "First" church, continue to be relevant and have a dynamic growing Sunday school after 170 years of existence? Are the principles that Houston's First Baptist employed to keep their Sunday school a relevant and effective ministry transferable to other churches regardless of the age, size, or location of the church?

Bill Hybels once said, "There is no such thing as a growing church." He meant that if you look at the long history of a church, no church consistently grows every year, year after year. There are seasons of advance and seasons of retreat. There are seasons to re-dream the dream. What got you here won't always get you there. Some churches that are great churches will go through periods of rapid growth, and then the growth slows although they can still have a significant impact in the community. After a while, they may have another strong season of growth. Some churches that once were strong and were reaching people begin to stagnate and eventually plateau like the vast majority of congregations and never regain the powerful witness, energy, and excitement that once characterized them. Why? Most of those churches have stopped doing church the way they once did. The key among those changes is that almost without exception, their Sunday school no longer functions according to the principles that it was designed to accomplish. Houston's First Baptist provides a great example of how a church can overcome the slumps, seasons, and changes of leadership to get back on track and continue making progress in effective ministry.

## BACK TO THE BEGINNING

Houston's First Baptist Church started in the very early years when Houston, Texas was barely a frontier town. The congregation can trace its heritage and family tree back to when missionary Elder Zachariah Morrell came from Tennessee to preach and minister in the new Republic of Texas. In his journal he wrote, "Houston, in 1837, was a city of tents; only one or two log-cabins appeared ... Plenty of 'John Barley Corn' and cigars. ... Upon inquiry I was informed that there never had been a sermon preached in the place."[1] He quickly remedied this by finding a cool place (it was early spring) and commencing to preach to an "attentive audience."

Within four years, the group of believers that continued to gather for prayer and worship with various preachers and missionaries formed Houston's First Baptist Church. The historical record of the church reads, "It was, in all actuality, a series of distant events which eventually led to the organization of First Baptist Church.... As planned, the first permanent organization

---

1. Kate Atkinson Bell, Christine Hall Ladner, Joanna Williams Poor, and Mona Petronella, *A Church in the City Reaching the World* (Houston, TX: D. Armstrong Co. Inc., 1985), 4.

was perfected on April 10, 1841, and the first official minutes of the First Baptist Church in Houston were recorded."[2]

To the point and context of this book, an early part of the congregation's strategy was to form and conduct a weekly Sunday school. Sunday school is first mentioned in the minutes of First Baptist Church in 1846, "as the church prepared to move into its first building." Mr. and Mrs. T. B. Hadley moved to Houston from Mississippi in 1840 and were instrumental in establishing the first organized Sunday school at First Baptist Church.

Dr. J. B. Link, pastor from 1867–69, saw the vision and value of a church employing the growing movement among churches known as Sunday school. "The Church gained much stability through its association with Reverend Link. ... [H]e perfected an effective organization for doing systematic church work throughout the city. ... The membership was organized into groups to look after visitors, Sunday school, missions, relief, and prayer service throughout the city."[3] In 1866, at the newly organized Baptist State Sunday School Convention of Texas, Dr. Link was an influential part of the program and revealed his deep interest in the matter. In 1869, Dr. Link wrote his views in the *Texas Baptist Herald,* the first Baptist state paper, "Sunday school work in Texas is only beginning to be appreciated. Even ministers seem but feebly to realize the momentous importance of this great work."[4]

In the early 1920s, "First Baptist Church was successful in following through with the Southern Baptist Convention's Sunday School Board plans and became the first organized adult Sunday school department in the Southern Baptist Convention."[5]

---

2.    Ibid, 5.
3.    Ibid, 22.
4.    Ibid, 124.
5.    Ibid.

However, First Baptist has gone through periods of advance and stagnation. "Sunday school attendance was at its lowest point, until early 1970, when Dr. John Bisagno became pastor. Harry Piland came to First Baptist in 1973. . . . He was very effective in guiding the mushrooming Sunday school and church attendance into an efficient graded and completely staffed organization."[6] Remember this last sentence, because it is the key to any church regaining its footing and growth.

## THE BLESSINGS OF A SUNDAY SCHOOL IN TIMES OF TRANSITION

Sunday school flourishes most when all key components of ministry are present and are functioning at a level of excellence. A church, undoubtedly, needs strong pastoral leadership, solid biblical preaching, a spiritually mature congregation working in harmony, an excellent worship and praise ministry, mature believers giving obediently, and, of course, a strong dynamic small group strategy. However, the Sunday school ministry is such an effective and strong tool that even when other essential elements of the church aren't present or aren't functioning at an optimum level, the Sunday school can continue to grow and have a major impact in helping to sustain the congregation as a church through a slump or staff changes.

Houston's First Baptist experienced this firsthand when Dr. John Bisagno retired after a strong and effective thirty-one-year ministry. The church entered a four-and-a-half-year search for a new pastor. At the same time of Dr. Bisagno's retirement, four other senior staff retired or resigned—leaving Dr. David Self, then the minister of education, with the weight of the church on his shoulders. Dr. Self, currently the executive pastor, has written a spiritually rewarding and insightful book about that transitional period titled, *Church Work Rules*. In it he shares

---

6.    Ibid, 125.

the experiences of leading the church during the interim and how God helped sustain him and Houston's First Baptist in those days. During a prolonged period without a senior pastor, four permanent senior staff vacancies, and tremendous indebtedness, the Lord blessed the church by not only keeping them on course and together but also actually bringing growth for the first time in years. There were several spiritual key elements used by God during that time. I do not diminish the impact of strong godly leadership and a mature body of believers seeking to follow God's will for the church; however, you cannot overlook the blessing of a having a solid, well-organized Sunday school ministry during such a period in the life a church. Of course, God used many key leaders and events to lead the church through this transitional period in their history. But the fact that the Sunday school attendance actually increased by more than two hundred during that time affirms that progress can occur whether your church is well-established, or you are navigating through seasons of change and challenge.

Today, guided by senior pastor Gregg Matte, Houston's First Baptist is on the verge of surpassing all of the high-water marks of her impressive history. Worship attendance, Life Bible Study, (a.k.a. Sunday school) attendance, baptisms, giving, and missions work are all continuing to increase in a long established setting. A church can truly re-dream the dream if grounded with strong godly leadership that follow key principles of ministry. For the purpose of this study, let's look at the key principles that have enabled HFBC to recapture her "best days" in her past.

## KEY FACTORS THAT ALLOW AN ESTABLISHED SUNDAY SCHOOL TO EXCEL

**First, know what the purpose of your Sunday school is, and stick to it.** In all my work with other churches and talking with scores of church leaders, not fully understanding the purpose of one's Sunday school ministry is one of the main reasons most of our Sunday schools aren't growing as they should. Indeed, I will go further to say that I believe lacking purpose in Sunday school is why so many church leaders have looked elsewhere for a strategy for discipleship and church growth, leading many to pronounce Sunday school as a thing of the past. For years I have asked church leaders, conference attendees, and even those staff members charged with Bible study and discipleship, "What is the purpose of Sunday school?," and I am not exaggerating when I say that most have not had a clear understanding. Often, the understanding of what they are trying to accomplish with their Sunday school ministry is misguided and muddy.

Purpose is important if you want to accomplish the task. I have a favorite illustration I like to use with groups I am speaking to that makes the point. I will ask them, "What is the purpose of a hammer?" Of course, they all get it, to drive in nails. Then I ask, "What is the purpose of a screwdriver?" Again they all get it, and by now are looking at me like, "Wow, you're really deep." Then I ask how many have ever tried to put a screw in a wall with a hammer because a screwdriver wasn't available and vice-versa? Most laugh and agree; they have done both. Then I ask, "How effective was it?" You get the point, I'm sure. Of course, you can drive a screw into a wall with a hammer and hammer a nail with the handle of a screwdriver, but the results aren't very pretty. It's not very effective, and there is always collateral damage along the way like marred walls, smashed fingers, and most importantly nails or screws that are weak and do not effectively do the job intended. The point is that Sunday school is a powerful tool, and is your most powerful tool *when* organized and used for the purpose for which it is intended. However, when we use it for less than intended, or even with a misguided purpose, then it is not effective and like the nails and screws in the illustration, it is weak.

This begs the question then, "What is the purpose?" Did you notice in the brief history of Houston's First Church that the purpose was always clear and to the point? In the written history of

Houston's First Baptist Church, you will read on page 125, "For a church to consistently reach, teach, win and develop persons in the Christian faith it is imperative that it have an effective Sunday school organization."[7] Did you catch it? The purpose of the Sunday school as employed by those who want to use this ministry in its most effective and productive manner is to "reach, teach, win and develop persons in the Christian faith." For the most part, any version or restatement of the purpose of Sunday school will include, stated one way or the other, the task of reaching people, winning people to Christ, teaching them the Word of God, and developing or discipling the believers.

How has Houston's First Baptist been able to re-dream the dream and keep it alive through 170 years and going? It has always stayed with this purpose and focused the Sunday school ministry on reaching, teaching, winning, and disciple making. The Sunday school might have drifted from time to time or become overly focused on other issues, but every time it came back to that central purpose it recaptured the desire to grow and make a tremendous impact again. Just a little over four years ago HFBC's average Sunday school attendance had gone through another slump, but upon refocusing the staff and Sunday school leadership on the purpose, we have seen the weekly average attendance rebound and begin to grow once again. To be sure, there are some other key principles that have helped get our Sunday school back on track, but it started with our recommitting to the primary purpose of the Sunday school.

**The next step to revitalizing a Sunday school is making certain that the key leaders share a common understanding and agreement of the purpose of Sunday school.** To paraphrase Jim Collins in *Good to Great*, it is not about just getting the right people on the bus and the wrong people off the bus, it

---

7.    Ibid, 125.

is about teaching, mentoring, and leading your staff and leaders to see the purpose and to get on board the bus with you.

As important as it is to get the pastor and staff (when in a multi-staff context) on the same page, it is vital that the lay leadership of your Sunday school understand and buy into the purpose. They need to also be open to learning how to implement the purpose as a strategy in their group. You will need to invest much more time and effort into training on an individual level as well a group level.

It is not enough that the staff and volunteer leadership understand the purpose of the Sunday school. **The third key is to make sure the members of the Sunday school understand and accept the purpose.** I wish I had a nickel for every time a Sunday school leader has told me something to this effect, "I really want to help create a new class out of our group, but the members will not go along with it." When that happens, it reveals one of three things: you either have a leader that has not accepted the purpose and strategy of the Sunday school, you have a weak leader who is not leading his or her group, or you have a leader that has failed to lead the members to understand and accept the purpose of the Sunday school. I understand that this is a never-ending task, and you will never get everyone to buy in, but you can get enough members on board so that it will enable you to do what needs to be done to help the Sunday school grow.

**The next step is to keep the strategy of outreach and evangelism at the heart of the Sunday school.** From the very beginning of the Sunday school movement, a key element that made Sunday schools work so effectively has been keeping the focus of reaching and winning people to faith in Jesus Christ. In the last four years at Houston's First Baptist, we have recharged the Sunday school organization with a strong emphasis on both outreach and inreach. We are installing outreach and inreach leaders who serve with their care group leaders, and are charged with the task to minister and connect with guests and members in a more effective way. The point is that when any church places an emphasis on these key functions, organizes in a way to give priority to them, and commits to train the leaders, it has a tremendous impact on the Bible study ministry.

**Finally, train and equip your leadership to do the work of the Sunday school.** A well thought-out strategy to train leadership must always be in place if you want to revitalize or keep your Sunday school energized. You cannot neglect equipping as a strategy and expect any of the concepts I have described to be embraced or implemented. Failure to train will inevitably lead to a loss of focus, and ultimately to a Sunday school ministry that flounders.

Houston's First Baptist has always placed a high priority on regular leadership meetings. All of the leadership luncheons and training events are designed to keep the leaders not only informed but also motivated. In the last four years, we have placed renewed emphasis on training with a special emphasis on a major annual training event that is highly promoted, prepared, and participated in by the leaders. The key to making the training work is to get buy-in from the most influential leaders, development of a good format, strong guest leaders who are practitioners, early and excellent promotion, and of course, lots of hard work.

## SUNDAY SCHOOL STILL WORKS WHEN YOU WORK THE SUNDAY SCHOOL

I firmly believe and have experienced the truth that Sunday school works when you work it. I often tell groups of church leaders that Sunday school works every time it is tried, as long as you adhere to the purpose and are committed as a leader to make it work. I have shared some of the key steps that have helped Houston's First Baptist to continue re-dreaming the dream for over 170 years! Our story, while perhaps unique because of our age, is not unlike other great churches. I know of churches of all sizes that are committed to making their Sunday school an effective tool in the twenty-first century. If you give an honest evaluation of the various methods to reach people, teach the Word, evangelize your community, and begin people on a healthy path to discipleship, you will see that much like the report that Mark Twain read of his death, the report of the death of Sunday school has been greatly exaggerated.

# CHAPTER 5

# Excels with a Small Congregation

## J. D. "Sonny" Tucker

FARMERVILLE IS A BEAUTIFUL SMALL town sitting on one of the most popular fishing lakes in Northeast Louisiana. Lake D'Arbonne is the destination of anglers from across the south and also happens to be in the proximity of a church that has a Sunday school that really excels. The lake is known far and wide, but those who live locally are also aware of the Beulah Baptist Church led by Pastor Jeff Hurst. One would have to travel out into the country from Monroe or Bastrop to find Farmerville, and even farther out in the parish and down a paved country road to find Beulah Baptist Church.

The success of the Sunday school at Beulah is significant on several levels. First and foremost would be that their growth is significant in its own right. Each number represented by their growth represents a person that is exceedingly special and loved by our Lord. A number is not a number for numbers sake. A number is a real person such as a child, grandparent, spouse, or friend. Secondly, Beulah has excelled in spite of the fact that they are not located on a highly visible piece of property. That merits close study of the dynamics of their blessing and growth. Thirdly, they are not a large congregation with an abundance of staff and resources, thus making the principles and practices that have brought them success all the more important. Finally, demographics of the area do not reveal a large number of new people moving into the area that can provide a church with an influx of believers from other states or regions. Transfer growth can often serve to enhance the attendance in the church that is blessed to be located in a growing community. That means Beulah has to reach those who are already there. Many leaders in circumstances such as these would suggest that "we have no prospects." Beulah, however, chooses to reach out to the population that God has placed within their reach.

The number of smaller membership churches in the United States and Canada are ubiquitous (an Arkansas term meaning there are a whole bunch of them). In the Arkansas Baptist State Convention alone there are 1,100 out of 1,550 churches and missions that average one hundred or less in Sunday school attendance, with 874 of those averaging fifty or less. Many of these churches are in areas of low population density and in locations of diminished visibility. These factors in no way decrease the value and importance of these congregations to the kingdom, but merely present unique challenges to these churches. Many of these smaller or rural church pastors would say that much of the literature on church health and Sunday school growth would mainly target larger congregations in an urban or suburban bedroom community setting. Thus any growth principles that may be extracted from a rural church in a no-population-growth setting, and applied to other congregations in similar contexts, would be extremely valuable and beneficial.

Enter Beulah Baptist Church, Farmerville, Louisiana, as a great model of a church in a rural, no-population-growth area that has experienced significant blessing and growth. Statistical data reveals that Beulah has grown in the last few years from fifty-nine to 101 in average Sunday school attendance and from eighty-five to 120 in worship attendance. The church has experienced profound blessing and growth while being located in a rural, no-population-growth setting.

When you meet Pastor Jeff Hurst, you instantly like him. He is humble, kind, unselfish, unassuming, yet driven with a passion for God and a love for people. He is quick and relentless in giving God all the glory and credit for the great things that have transpired at Beulah Baptist Church. Jeff is a native of the area, so he is keenly aware of its context, culture, preferences, challenges, and strengths. He knows it is a great privilege to be able to minister in the area in which you were raised. He knows these people, and he fits in with them.

## FOUR KEY OVERARCHING AREAS OF FOCUS

Pastor Jeff clearly articulates the factors that he believes are behind the miracle at Beulah. He believes that in a setting like this the Sunday school must not be a stand-alone or isolated organization. Rather, it must partner with and undergird every part of the church's ministry. Pastor Jeff focuses on four things that have deeply impacted the Sunday school and ministries of Beulah.

First, a major focus is on direct, intentional evangelism. Outreach is not merely discussed at Beulah; it is taught and practiced. There are two primary evangelistic methods employed by Beulah. The first is attractional harvest events. At these events, non-church attendees are invited to activities sponsored by the church where the gospel is shared and people are given an opportunity to respond to the claims of Christ. These events are often age-targeted and come in various forms, but they are ever-present at Beulah. The second evangelistic method employed by Beulah is personally inviting people to church and simultaneously giving them a business-card-sized information piece with directions, service times, and a brief plan of salvation. Pastor Jeff has found that a warm and sincere personal invitation to church carries significant meaning to those invited. This passion and focus on evangelism spills over into everything that the Sunday school does.

A second key area of focus for Pastor Jeff is having a warm and loving fellowship in the church. Pastor Jeff believes most churches talk about this but few achieve it. The spirit of love, warmth, and compassion must first exist in a believer's heart because of their authentic relationship with Jesus Christ. This should precipitate a deep, unselfish, and committed love within the church among the members. As a result, this deep compassion can and should flow out into meaningful expressions to those who do not attend church. Pastor Jeff believes strongly in the old adage "people don't care how much you know until they know how much you care." Area residents know that Pastor Jeff and Beulah really care about people and continually seek to meet needs. Their compassion is so deep and great that it has a major impact on the community. It is a normal practice for the church to pray over people who have significant burdens. Whether in Sunday school or worship service, it is common to have people needing prayer to sit in a chair and the members gather around them and pray. The church is also actively involved in assisting people in the community during times of crisis. This ranges from simply being there when people have a need to taking up a special collection for certain needs. Pastor Jeff says the church places a priority on "toting each other's burdens" when life gets difficult.

The third key area of focus for Beulah is prayer. Pastor Jeff emphasizes and practices times of prayer that are focused and intense. Influenced by the writings and ministries of E. M. Bounds and Leonard Ravenhill, Jeff Hurst understands the need for prayer and personal spiritual revival. The power behind the Sunday school ministry of the church is the prayer of the people.

The fourth area of focus for Beulah Baptist Church is the guest ministry. There is intentionality and intensity in the follow-up of guests. Guests are viewed by this congregation and by Pastor Jeff as special gifts from God. Jeff leads the members to make immediate contact with guests and to follow up their visit to the church. It would be unthinkable to Jeff that someone would visit the church seeking spiritual direction, and not receive a follow-up contact. Pastor Jeff and the church are cognizant of the fact that people are attracted to places where they are valued and affirmed. This value and appreciation for guests must move beyond mere feelings of the heart to practical, tangible expressions like a phone call, email, or personal visit. These follow-up contacts are not comprised of heavy-handed guilt or coercion, but rather expressions of appreciation and statements of the guest's value to the church and to God.

## TRANSFERRING KEY PRINCIPLES TO SUNDAY SCHOOL

The principles that are so predominant in Beulah Church spill over into the Sunday school and have significant impact on it. As stated previously, the Sunday school organization is not a stand-alone organization at Beulah but rather a microcosm of the church as a whole. Beulah Baptist Church successfully transfers these principles to the Sunday school so that they are fleshed out in the context of small groups. The influence of these principles affects the Sunday school in six specific ways.

The first key to the success of the Sunday school at Beulah Baptist Church is the regular teachers' meetings. Sunday school teachers are viewed as some of the most important and impacting leaders in the church. Because of the extreme value placed on them, Pastor Jeff yields much personal time and effort to support and undergird their work. Every Sunday evening while the church members meet in discipleship classes, Pastor Jeff has a class for the Sunday school teachers. He leads the class personally with several goals in mind. First is simply to encourage the teachers. He expresses verbally what they mean to him, the church's ministry, and to the kingdom. It is constantly placed before these teachers that the small group ministry is of vital importance to the church. The teachers understand that church attenders are never really assimilated into the life of the church until they are involved in a small group of some kind. And the small group ministry that is the easiest to move guests into is the Sunday school. It is impacting to these teachers to walk away every Sunday night having their personal service and their organization valued and affirmed.

The Bible study for them for the following week serves as a primary subject in the leadership meetings. Each class uses the same curriculum, so the theme and focus is the same regardless of the age divisions. Pastor Jeff covers the main themes, key phrases, intent, and scope of the lesson. This gives the teachers a jump start on their personal preparation as they study and pray over the content throughout the week.

A second aspect of the teacher's meeting is training on how to effectively teach the lesson and how to effectively minster through the Sunday school. The teachers discuss problem areas and difficult spots that they may be encountering. This group discussion, brainstorming, and wisdom-sharing have proven extremely effective to the teachers.

Another important aspect of the teachers' meeting is the prayer time. The prayer time is not merely an add-on appendage or "lite-duty" prayer, but rather one of the most important keys to the teacher's meetings and the Sunday school as a whole. The group prays for the needs of the class members, for those who have yet to make a personal faith decision, for power during the class time, and for life change. Pastor Jeff states that this time of prayer is often emotional and lengthy. It often amounts to "revival every Sunday night" among the teachers.

The next aspect of the success of the Sunday school at Beulah is the pastor's involvement. Pastor Jeff is personally a good Sunday school class member. Though he may visit each class to fellowship before they officially begin, he ends up in his own particular group as a regular and active participant.

Pastor Jeff also promotes the Sunday school regularly and consistently from the pulpit. He is keenly aware that what he promotes from the pulpit transfers to the church members as priority to the church. He conveys to guests, and to those who only attend the worship service, the importance and blessing of being involved in the small group ministry of the church. Jeff Hurst understands that a church that is built around the preaching ministry of the pastor and not the small groups will only be strong as long as the pastor is serving there.

Another explanation for the success of the Sunday school at Beulah Church is that they assertively go after the worship service guests in an attempt to connect them to the Sunday school. Jeff Hurst understands that the most productive prospects that exist for the Sunday school are the new guests to the worship service and those whom regularly attend worship services but not Sunday school. The church believes that the best vehicle to move folks from merely being worship service attendees to Sunday school members is to connect them to Sunday school class members. Personal invitations to Sunday school, class fellowships, and lunch after church work well. The church is very cognizant that guest follow-up is a major priority for Pastor Jeff personally.

Their contact will be in addition to the pastor's personal contact and will enhance the warmth and welcome felt by the guest. Beulah Church members understand that prospects merely seeking a worship service or top-quality Bible teaching can get it via televised worship services every Sunday morning. If they pass up these great speakers and attend a local church they are seeking more than just a sermon. They are seeking friends and a faith family with whom to partner while walking through life. Because Beulah really cares about people, and because they consistently express it through words and actions, they have provided a fertile climate for growth.

A final reason for the success of the Sunday school at Beulah is that they practice good, solid Sunday school growth principles—especially those of providing space and starting new groups. Space requirements and new class procedures, found in any standard Sunday school guide, are followed at Beulah. The church added worship space and classrooms onto their existing building when they began to run out of space. By doing solid Sunday school work, caring and connecting to people, and adding space and new groups, the church has overcome the typical pattern of people merely joining but not connecting. The numbers bear out the fact that the normal pattern is for people to join this congregation and to become active participants.

This brief assessment of Beulah Baptist Church in Farmerville, Louisiana, spells out their base plan for accomplishing their Kingdom assignment. Though the church is well-known in northeast Louisiana, it is no accident that they have been so blessed. Their fame is earned because they work hard and focus on the tasks that matter most. The commitment to these priorities has enabled them to excel with a small congregation. Small congregations can thrive because God is not limited by numbers of population, but can guide any church to excel where he has placed them.

# CHAPTER 6

# Excels in Hands-on Missions

## *Bob Mayfield*

IT WAS A COLD, LATE-WINTER morning as my pastor and I had breakfast in a local restaurant. After some small talk, we began wrestling with the issue that many churches and pastors face, "How do we get our people out of the pews and into the community around our church?" It is one of the most frustrating issues a pastor faces. Church members will sit in a class and occupy a pew for years and never engage a neighbor, colleague, or friend with the gospel. As my pastor and I talked over our eggs, bacon, and several cups of coffee, we began to write our thoughts on some napkins.

Before I finish my story, have you ever considered the true purpose of Sunday school? I lead the Sunday school organization of our state convention, and I often have the privilege of leading Sunday school training seminars for church leaders. As I train pastors, Sunday school directors, and teachers at these seminars, I usually start by asking a simple question. "What is the purpose of Sunday school?" Invariably the following three answers are the most common:

- Bible study
- Ministry
- Fellowship

Although all three of these topics are a vital part of Sunday school, none of them are the purpose of Sunday school. Bible study, ministry, and fellowship are three of the activities that we engage our people so that we can accomplish our true mission—making disciples of Jesus Christ.

Furthermore, I prefer not to identify Sunday school as a ministry or program of the church. In reality, Sunday school is a strategy. I define Sunday school as the church's primary strategy to connect people to Jesus, his community, his truth, and his mission. Essentially, Sunday school is how the church is organized to carry out its mission. For a Sunday school to truly excel in mission, the people in the Sunday school and especially the church leadership must understand what the true mission of the church and the Sunday school really is.

A Sunday school that excels in mission is a Sunday school that is committed to making disciples through a small group strategy for the purpose of putting each member of the church on the mission field—be it at work, school, across the street, or around the world. For most churches, the Sunday school is the largest organization of the church. It should make sense that the largest organization of the local church should be the most committed to the mission of the church. For a Sunday school to accomplish its mission, it must actively and purposely excel in five connections.

First, it must connect with people. Sunday school is not intended to be an institutional exercise that a church does on Sunday morning in connection with a corporate worship service. Instead, Sunday school is an intentional effort to connect with people relationally. Its ultimate purpose is to make disciples by leading each person to faith in Christ and bringing each person to spiritual maturity. This intentional connection is better done in the context of a small group network of relationships.

Secondly, the intention of Sunday school must be about connecting people to a personal, saving relationship with Jesus Christ. A Sunday school that excels is evangelistic at its core. Members of the group have relationships with friends who do not know Christ as Lord. The group is a natural place to introduce someone to the person of Christ in an environment where the individual can learn and experience the gospel.

The third connection is connecting people to God's community, the church. Sunday school has a rich tradition of being outstanding in connecting people into the church family. Because it is relational in nature, the small group dynamic of Sunday school connects people in community where they can receive prayer and personal care. Research by Thom Rainer reveals that eighty-six percent of people who accept Christ and become involved in Sunday school will still be active in church five years later. If a person is only connected through worship, the number falls to fourteen percent.[1]

A fourth connection that must be made in a Sunday school that excels is to connect people to God's truth—the Bible. From its earliest days of teaching children how to read to the present, Sunday school is perhaps most synonymous with Bible study. A Sunday school that excels is connecting people to life changing Bible study. God's Word is sharper than a two-edged sword and is able to pierce the souls of men (Heb. 4:12). Our world today tries to take the edge off of truth and dull the blade. Worldly truth is constantly being adjusted to suit our purpose. But Hebrews 4:12 specifically states that the truth has a sharp edge to it. Sunday school is a place where people can have a

---

1. Thom Rainer, *Surprising Insights from the Unchurched* (Grand Rapids, MI: Zondervan, 2001), 119–120.

transformational experience each week through the application of God's Word to their life.

As my pastor and I shared our thoughts with each other while we drank our coffee and scribbled on our napkins, an idea began to emerge. Like many other churches, when the church sent a mission team somewhere, only a handful of people would actually go on the mission. Many people in our church would give money to support the team, and we all enjoyed hearing their stories when they returned home. That is when we came to the realization: Our church was experiencing missions vicariously. Few of our members were personally on mission, but we felt that we were because we all knew and supported someone who had been on mission.

We had a thought. Is there some way that we could get our entire church family on mission together in our community? This is where the fifth and final connection is made: A Sunday school excels by getting its people involved in God's mission. My pastor and I had thought: What if we asked every Sunday school class in the church to do a mission project during the spring? What would be the impact in our community if our church members (average attendance—220) would go on mission together?

Pastor Mark called a meeting of our church's Sunday school leaders and explained the process to them. We asked our Sunday school groups to complete some type of mission project over the course of the spring. On the first Sunday of May, he announced that we were going to have a Mission Celebration at the church and share what God had done through us in our community. Every class in the church accepted the challenge.

Let me share the experience of the group that I attend. Our teacher, brother Dale, shared the idea with our group. After sharing the concept, Dale shared two more thoughts with us that really affected the outcome of our group. First, he wanted our group's mission project to take place in the community around our church facility. Second, Dale challenged our group to go beyond packing a shoebox full of socks and toothpaste. To be clear, none of us have a problem with ministries that deliver shoeboxes of hope all over the world, but for this kind of project our group could do more. We wanted a project that our entire group could get hands-on with, and we did.

We connected with a needy family in our community. My wife, myself, and another lady in our group agreed to meet this family and look for opportunities where we could minister to them. Ministry opportunities were abundant. We met a mother and her daughter, Julie and Marie (not their real names) at their trailer home. Light fixtures in the ceiling had water pooling in them from the leaky roof. The skirting around the trailer was in shambles and wild animals often spent the night under their home. The steps to the deck were rotten and the trailer was in dire need of some paint. In response to our question of how we could help them, Julie asked if we could fix the doors on her home so that they would close and lock.

Our report to our Sunday school class also included that this little family survived (barely) on a $400 a month government subsidy. The rent on their trailer was $300. The class responded to this opportunity with enthusiasm. We set a date for everyone to meet at Julie and Marie's home and do some much needed repairs. Our scouting trip also revealed something else: Julie and Marie live outside of town and their propane tank was empty. They had gone most of the winter without heat.

At this point, let me share some information with you about our group. We had nineteen people enrolled in our group, and our average attendance is usually around twelve. We are a group of people in their late forties and early fifties, and our children are generally in high school or young adults. We began collecting the money that we would need to do the necessary repairs and also fill the five-hundred-gallon tank with propane. Our group met for our workday at Julie and Marie's, and all nineteen of us showed up. We patched the roof and completely replaced the skirting around the trailer. We applied a coat of paint and repaired the steps leading up to the front deck. In addition, we also completely reframed both of the outside doors and put new doors on the trailer that were sturdy and had new locks on them. The more work we did, the more we discovered additional work that needed to be done. We had people traveling to and from the nearest hardware store all day.

Because we are Baptists, and therefore like to eat, one of our couples brought a grill. Julie and Marie did not have any neighbors nearby, but there were a number of other houses and mobile homes within a half mile. One of our group members hastily made some invitations, and we sent a team of people to invite the neighbors over for hamburgers and hot dogs. Three neighboring families showed up about noon. We ate with them, and the work we were doing on Julie and Marie's home gave us an opportunity to tell them about our church and Jesus Christ.

Our group finished our work on that Saturday. Sunday morning we excitedly gathered together for our Bible study but Julie, Marie, or any of the other families we had met the previous day did not show up for church. They did not show up the next Sunday either, or the next. However, our experience with Julie and Marie was not over. Our group fell in love with this sweet family. Julie was unemployed and had no marketable job skills. Her daughter Marie is slightly mentally challenged. What started as a one day mission project became an ongoing ministry opportunity for us to share the love of Christ with this precious family.

Only a few weeks following our workday at their home, Julie's brother passed away. She called to see if our group could help her with some gas money so that she could attend the funeral. Our group had seen the family car and it was not roadworthy. One of our members took Julie to a rental car agency, rented her a car for the trip and gave her $200 for gas. The men in our group signed up to take turns keeping the lot around their home mowed.

It was one day in August when it was my turn to mow the lot. While mowing it, Julie asked me if I wanted some iced tea when I was done. I went to their deck for the tea, and her daughter Marie came out—in a brand new set of clothes. Marie is mainstreamed and attends a rather wealthy school. One of the ladies in our group took Marie to the mall and bought her five brand new sets of clothes so that she would have something different to wear to school every day.

A couple of weeks later, we dismissed from our Sunday school class and walked into the auditorium to attend worship. There on the front row sat Julie and Marie. Apparently, they did not realize the Baptists fill a room from the back to the front. Four months after our workday at their home, they came to worship. Our group sat beside them—on the front row.

Later in the year, Julie contacted my wife and another lady in our group and asked them if they would sit with her in a court room. The reason they were so insistent on having the doors to their trailer repaired became evident. Marie was testifying against a man who had broken into their trailer and assaulted her, and Julie needed support with her as she sat in the courtroom to watch her daughter give testimony.

As a result of our pastor's passion to engage our church members in putting the gospel on display in our community, we had all of our Sunday school classes participate. Even the bed babies had a mission (the teachers collected baby formula for needy moms). Our two- and three-year-old department collected nursery items and delivered them to a crisis pregnancy center. A children's group gathered backpacks for needy school children and another group did a home makeover for a neighborhood widow. We asked each Sunday school class to share with us the number of people that were involved in their group's mission project. The total: One hundred eighty-six people out of our average attendance of 220 were involved in missions that year.

I realize that not every mission effort is going to have the same results that our group and our church experienced. Should your group choose to conduct a mission project, you may have people refuse your help. You will have people accept your help and then have nothing to do with you anymore. Your good intentions are going to be misconstrued. Some people you meet are going to look at you with scorn. Possibly, you may have people in your own church or group scoff at the idea of helping those outside of the church. You may hear, "If they need us, they know where to find us." Let me share some advice:

Do it anyway.

Our world needs to see that God's love is unconditional. When we offer love and help to people who cannot reciprocate, we are offering unconditional love. The world is very well acquainted with conditional, "I'll help you if you help me" kind of love. They need to see the church as a place where we will help you even if you hate us for doing it.

Many people who are far from God are also skeptical about the local church. They see our nice buildings and the nice cars that are parked there on Sundays. They see us take care of each other and spend money on our programs. But what they often do not see is the local church meeting the needs of its community. Your church and more specifically, your group, needs to put the gospel on display in your community. Remember, Sunday school is how the church is organized to do its mission. So let's do it!

We have people who have sat in Sunday school and worship services for years. We have all listened to sermons and lessons about missions and evangelism. In many ways, our churches are suffering from a failure to launch. Let me encourage your group to connect its members with their mission. You can play it safe and stay in the confines of the church facilities, or you can step out into your neighborhood and put the gospel on display. There are forty miracles in the book of Acts. Of those miracles, thirty-nine of them take place where the lost people are. Your group should excel at putting people on mission for God.

# CHAPTER 7

# Excels on the Heels of a Crisis

## David Francis and Sam Galloway

A TIME OF CRISIS CAN "make or break" a church and its Sunday school ministry. A crisis might be economic, like many churches in the opening decade of the twenty-first century have experienced. A crisis might be one of leadership. Occasionally key leaders fall, fail, or leave, almost always unexpectedly. Sometimes a crisis is caused by unexpected fallout from the implementation of bold new ideas.

When a church faces a crisis, perhaps the number-one challenge is resisting the temptation to go into survival mode. Don't change anything. Don't try anything new. Certainly do not attempt anything dramatic. Focus on maintaining what is in hand. Get your bearings. Take it slowly. Allow us to introduce you to a church that defied the conventional wisdom and actually excelled during a crisis by revamping its approach to ongoing Sunday morning Bible study groups.

Before the "Great Recession" hit, most of the United States at the end of the first decade of the twenty-first century, such as the Dayton, Ohio area, was already experiencing tough economic times. First Baptist Church, Vandalia, Ohio, was dealing with the impact of that economic crisis when her pastor led the church to refocus its Sunday school ministry on proven small group principles and an orientation toward outreach and community service. Just after the launch of the new strategy, the pastor of thirty-one years, Dr. Charles Betts, suffered a massive stroke that eventually took his life. How does a church that experiences a period of crisis not only keep things going, but also actually grow? For First Baptist Vandalia, the sustaining factor was a revamped and refocused Sunday school ministry.

## A PASTOR'S HEART

Long-term pastor Charles D. Betts had a heart and a passion to reach northwest Dayton for Christ. Nearing the age of seventy, after thirty years as pastor of First Baptist, Dr. Betts inspired the church to continue moving forward. He led the church to consider its strategic location to the community high school and encouraged them to build a state-of-the-art activity center to minister to those students. The facility—very near Dayton International Airport, home of many air shows dating back to the time of the Wright Brothers—is aptly called "The Hanger."

At the dedication of The Hanger, Pastor Betts shared a testimony about meeting some skateboarders. They were doing "grinders" on the brand new concrete parking curbs. Dr. Betts went over to talk with the boys and said, "I'm glad you are using the church parking lot. Don't worry if you chip some of the concrete. All that can be fixed. I want you to know that we have plans to build a proper place for you to skateboard right over there. We'll have rails and half-pipes for you to use." When asked about his remarks, Dr. Betts said, "We work hard to get folks to come to church, so we can reach them. These boys have come here voluntarily, and we need to demonstrate a reason they should keep coming, so we can help them see Jesus in us."

While paving the way for transitioning to the next generation by leading the church to build The Hanger, the pastor
set a course of encouraging the reorganization of the Sunday
school to use small group principles of reaching out, growing
in community, and caring. A staff study group used Hal Mayer's
*Making the Critical Connection: Combining the Best of Small
Group Dynamics with Sunday School* to analyze and personalize the purpose and organization of their Sunday school. The
reorganization was launched in March 2007 as "small groups"
meeting on Sunday morning and using ongoing Bible study
materials from LifeWay Christian Resources.

## OBSTACLES AND OPPORTUNITIES

The week following the implementation of the new strategy,
Pastor Betts suffered a massive stroke to which he succumbed
about five months later. Yet despite the trauma to the church,
the reorganized ongoing Bible study groups proved to be effective, and the church was blessed with more baptisms in the two
months after the March 2007 reorganization. Amazingly, that
occurred while the church prayed for the senior pastor in the
critical-care unit.

Dr. Betts realized over the years that his Sunday school leaders had forgotten why they were doing what they were doing.
The Sunday school had fallen prey to the notion that the purpose was primarily for "going deeper into the Word" (which,
being translated, means "the teacher lectures the attendees").
Most groups were stagnant with very few class fellowships,
very little emphasis on growth, not much genuine caring beyond cordiality, and absolutely no sense of mission.

A group of key leaders was assembled to evaluate and
recommend a course for revitalization. *Making the Critical
Connection* by Hal Mayer was used by the team as a resource to
guide the strategy. The book is based on the story of Flamingo
Road Church in Fort Lauderdale, Florida, which experienced

explosive growth by transitioning to a hybrid model that combined the best elements of Sunday school with the best elements of relational small groups.

Some reorganizational suggestions were added or modified by FBC Vandalia to make the restructuring plan workable in their context. The planning, discussions, training, and communication of the planned changes took place over a span of six months.

### *A Crisis at Launch*

If you've ever witnessed a space shuttle mission, you know that the most dangerous—and occasionally tragic—periods are launch and reentry. Tragically, Pastor Betts suffered a massive stroke the week following the renewal launch. He was in intensive care for several weeks, made a partial recovery for a short time, but finally arrived in heaven. He pastored FBC Vandalia, Ohio from 1976 until his death.

And yet, because of Dr. Betts's foresight, the church experienced a renewal of their Sunday school that resulted in people coming to faith in Jesus and the growth of the church. Ten new adult groups were launched during the time of the pastor's absence. That decision reduced the size of the existing groups but resulted in a total increase in overall attendance.

In addition, the church instituted a servant-leadership principle derived from Mayer's book that tripled the number of leaders involved in Sunday school. Each adult small group was trained to enlist six servant leaders: teacher, apprentice teacher (committed to developing skills and launching a new group in eighteen to twenty-four months), group coordinator, care group leader, outreach leader, and a party leader (whose job description emphasized that parties were intended primarily to encourage new prospects to join the small group). Outreach and party leaders work closely together. Care group leaders make sure they have group leaders who each care for seven members they contact regularly. The group coordinator manages the class schedule and activities.

At the two-month mark following the reorganization, the most important role in these small group leadership teams turned out to be the party leader. These leaders were responsible for attracting more new members to join small groups than any other factor. The staff points out that the group coordinator has become the most influential factor in maintaining a growing and thriving small group.

Along with the change in structure and purpose came a re-naming of Sunday school to "small groups," but the occasion and location remained the same. Small groups meet on Sunday mornings at Vandalia First Baptist Church.

### Sustaining the Launch

Part two of the church's Sunday morning Bible group renewal was the commitment to be sure new and prospective members had the information they needed to follow the simple goal FBC Vandalia has for them: Find God, Find Friends, Find a Job. To accomplish this simple three part goal, FBC Vandalia conducted a "First Impressions" meeting. All prospective members were invited to this two-hour meeting held after Sunday morning services. Lunch was provided and a special program was presented. Twenty guests were present at the first meeting.

The first subject of the "First Impressions" meeting was: Find God. Each participant was provided with a "First Impressions Membership Manual" that was produced by the church leaders for this element of the strategy. The first segment included introduction of church leadership, an overview of the church budget, and a presentation based on the Billy Graham tract "Steps to Peace with God." Everything presented was included in the manual. Prospective members were encouraged to take the manual home and to study it before they made a commitment to the church.

The second segment of the meeting was: Find Friends. Attendees were introduced at this point to the small group structure and goals. Attendees were oriented on how they could find friends in Sunday morning small groups. The focus of the final segment was: Find a Job. Participants were introduced to personality and spiritual gift assessment tools. These were to be completed and returned the following week.

What were the results of the first "First Impressions" meeting? Two adults trusted Jesus as Savior, and four of the twenty participants joined the church. The church continues to offer this program three to four times each year. The emphasis feeds new members into the Sunday school, helps prospective members connect more easily, and assists with identification of new leaders, which strengthens the overall ministry even more.

### *Keeping the Strategy Going*

What happened in the following months? Did the church revert to their former approach? FBC Vandalia persevered in its Spirit-led plans. Jean Cope, adult minister, reported one year later that "the church is still growing, and Sunday school reorganization is doing great even though the church is functioning under the leadership of an interim pastor." The church continued creating new groups, including a new young married group that resulted in twenty new people in attendance.

The reorganization did not take place without some resistance. One example was a senior men's group that refused to organize around the six recommended leadership roles. However, following a mission trip to Kentucky, the leader of the group returned with a renewed servant spirit and adopted the strategy. Jean reported furthermore that the church started two new classes: ESL and newly married. The newly married class was advertised for those married five years or less. The church has continued to add groups, and the result has not only increased attendance but also other ministries as well.

The Sunday morning small groups are the focus of the church's evangelism strategy, and the church continues to grow more than four years after the reorganization and the crisis.

## NEW PASTOR SUSTAINS THE STRATEGY

New pastors ordinarily introduce new ideas. That's not necessarily a crisis. It's just reality, so the church called someone to succeed Pastor Betts who not only embraced the strategy but also had been instrumental in forming it. Fourteen months after Dr. Betts died, the youth minister, David Starry, was called as lead pastor. He had served faithfully on the restructuring leadership team, then as Interim Pastor. He has helped continue to guide the church to grow, using the ongoing Sunday morning small group Bible study strategy. He continues to encourage the groups to engage in missions and ministry within the community. When they learned that thirty percent of local youth are underfed, the church developed a "backpack with food" ministry. A young-adult small group recruited to help in the "family food night" ministry has embraced the opportunity and has enlisted two other small groups to join them every third Monday. The restructuring and renewal of the "Sunday school" continues. It is a continual process.

### *Sunday School Can Excel in Pioneer Areas*

The Midwest is considered a "pioneer" area by our denomination because fewer evangelical congregations are present. Here are three quick illustrations of other "pioneer" area churches that have excelled using Sunday school and have continually experienced growth by adding new classes. The following reports were provided in 2011:

1. FBC, New Haven, IN: Added two new groups and attendance grew from 35 to 65 in one year, according to Pastor David Trimble.

2. Barrington Ridge BC, Hobart, IN: By encouraging one class of fifteen senior ladies to add a second class for the new second Sunday school hour, the attendance doubled for that age group alone. Jacob Lynch, the minister of education, pointed out that total attendance in Sunday school has increased from sixty-five to 140.

3. Hillcrest BC, Carlisle, OH: Six Sunday school classes were added last year and attendance increased from 280 to 350, according to church secretary Betty Terry.

The Barrington Ridge pastor, Mitch Whidden, shared this thought with me, "When I came to Hobart three years ago, I thought that I would have to establish a weekday small group strategy to reach people for Christ, but I found that the Sunday school model has been the most effective time and tool for reaching the families of northwest Indiana."

### Points of Application

First, it is essential for the pastor to support and encourage the purpose of Sunday school. The pastor has a team at his disposal but must be purposeful in engaging and equipping the Sunday school leaders. You can delegate some of the administration but must be seen as supportive and providing key leadership.

Secondly, administering Sunday school adds ministers. A healthy Sunday school does not function on autopilot. Attend to the organizational principles, and you can mobilize people in ministry and mission for Jesus Christ. Strong leaders are crucial to help in navigating crises in the church and may even help you avoid some potential problems. Grow leaders, and they will help you grow your Sunday school.

Finally, a crisis need not be a time to hit the brakes. It may be a time to push the accelerator. Certainly, it may be a time to revisit, reevaluate, or perhaps revitalize a great ministry for helping a church survive and thrive. Sunday schools can excel during the best of times, and can even give strength to your congregation in the midst of a crisis..

# CHAPTER 8

# Excels in Equipping Leaders

## *David Francis and Gary Jennings*

DO YOU HAVE ENOUGH LEADERS to do the right things the right way at the right time? Having asked that question many times, I've yet to hear an enthusiastic affirmative answer. Churches in general, and Sunday schools in particular, always need additional leaders as well as better equipped leaders, but they often settle for simply filling the gaps in the organization.

I am reminded of an actual story about "gap filling" shared with me several years ago about a young man who had just trusted Jesus as Savior during the invitation on a Sunday morning. Many churches have receiving lines where people who make spiritual decisions on Sunday morning stand in front of the congregation to be introduced to the church and, in some instances, voted on for membership. It is great for the congregation, but can be stressful for those who stand in front of everyone. On this particular Sunday morning, a young man responded to the invitation and gave his life to Jesus Christ. As he stood in the receiving line, a well-meaning gentleman shook his hand and asked him to begin teaching Sunday school to a group of boys. The new believer responded, "Teach them what?"

Approaching a newborn believer is not indicative of a healthy enlistment and equipping strategy. Church leaders usually mean well but don't always lead well. You need to discover, find, develop, and equip the right kind of leader to do the right job or ministry at the right time. Dunkirk Baptist Church in Dunkirk, Maryland is an example of a church that excels in equipping leaders.

## EQUIPPING LEADERS IN A MARYLAND CHURCH

Dunkirk Baptist Church is located in the suburban community of Dunkirk, Maryland, approximately thirty miles east-southeast of Washington, D.C. Dunkirk is a fast-growing community of mostly government workers who commute to and from the D.C. Beltway, near and around our nation's capital. The town is a place where the Potomac commuters can relax and enjoy a much slower pace of life. It provides a great balance to the hectic pace of work life that so many in the community are engaged in. Long commutes and long days at work present a huge challenge to Dunkirk Baptist church when it comes to enlisting, equipping, encouraging, and empowering leaders.

The church website states their goal to "help connect you with God and a local church community." The church is purposeful in seeking to create a climate of genuine friendship. They would agree that people are not simply looking for a friendly church, but are seeking friends. Dunkirk Church is committed to doing just that. They want to be friends to one another and to the community to which they are called to minister in Calvert County, Maryland. Why? So that the gospel is shared and lived out in relevant ways to a highly motivated Beltway commuter crowd who often do not have time for God. Some church attenders come to worship just to hear what God

is saying to them through the pastor because t̸
made time to hear from the Lord personally.

The Beltway is busy.

    The commute is horrendous.

    The pressure is constant.

Dunkirk Church needs highly motivated leaders to reach a segment of a population that is largely disconnected from spiritual things. Recently, a pastor of another D.C. Beltway church shared with me that his members "just want to come to church on Sunday morning, begging for the Word" because they didn't take time to meet with God during the week. Churches across America face similar challenges.

How do you go about enlisting leaders in such a geodemographic area? How do you equip them? How do you expect and equip leaders to excel in their church when they, themselves, want or need a break from the extremely high expectation environments they live in every day? Dunkirk was at one time a church satisfied with the status quo. A minimum of expectations were required of leaders, and the result was a decline in membership and attendance. The congregation came to a point of realization that decline will eventually lead to death if not remedied. They elected to focus and work toward a preferred future which could give them health and strength to impact their community. That future would require that they "Create a sustainable lay leadership team to direct the Sunday school discipleship process in our church." These words are found in their charter, and the mantra is more than a slogan to this congregation.

The journey to renewal began with the congregation praying for the right leaders instead of throwing names on the wall, like spaghetti, to see who sticks around to take the job. It started initially with the minister of education who kept calling individuals who might fill the vacant Sunday school director position. After several conversations and rejections, he began to lay his burden down and cry out to the Lord for a solution.

Pray? Had it come to that? Obviously, that is said with tongue in cheek, but many congregations are in the very same position. As he prayed, God answered, and the result was not one person but a team of four. Jesus prayed all night before he enlisted the apostles. He tells us to "pray the Lord of the harvest to send out laborers into His harvest" (Matthew 9:38). Prayer is not only spiritual but also practical, and essential to the enlistment and development of leaders.

The leadership team that was enlisted was empowered to seek any and all means to strengthen the Sunday school ministry. Teams often work better than individuals because of shared passion, vision, and sacrifice. The team is not a typical Sunday school team composed of a Sunday school director and age-division directors. They are four leaders who partner together along with the church staff to make the Sunday school ministry as effective as possible. The training began with the newly formed leadership team so that they could understand the dynamics of healthy Sunday school growth and ministry.

The team meets regularly and communicates weekly via email. They know the task at hand and work with all of the Sunday school leaders to bring it about. They meet periodically with the church staff to make sure they are on the same page. Sunday school has been relaunched by repurposing, by transitioning from a one-hour-a-week Bible study to a seven-day-a-week ministry. This means finding the right people to be on the proverbial bus of change. It has been exciting to see a care group ministry take shape and see that no one goes unnoticed or fails to receive ministry. Five new classes have been created in the past year in spite of the challenges required to do so. These priorities were not previously given sufficient attention. The result has been a ripple effect in the church in that other ministries are evaluating their purpose, structure, and effectiveness.

The leadership team and the minister of education went to work after completing their own training by inviting and

expecting all current Sunday school teachers to ga[
month to share in the vision of repurposing the current Sunday
school. Some leaders immediately embraced the new vision for
ministry, while others resisted and complained. Change was
in the air, and not every member desired change. The Sunday
school leadership team continued talking, communicating, en-
visioning, loving, and expecting the Sunday school teachers to
respond positively to the new direction. The expectation was
established that new people should be expected each and every
week. Attitudes slowly began shifting and transitioning because of the patience and perseverance of the leadership team.

The Sunday school leadership team knew they were going
to need more teachers, assistant teachers, and care group leaders, so they began a new process of interviewing potential
leaders with a ministry description in hand. The interviews included what was expected as well as why it was expected. Each
potential leader was oriented from the outset to understand the
purpose and meaning of his/her involvement in Sunday school.
The process was helpful in orienting, screening, and placing
candidates in a type of service. Not every person interviewed
by the team accepted leadership in Sunday school. However,
the experience enabled the leadership to assist them in identifying a place where they could serve and make a difference
whether as a Sunday school teacher, a Sunday school leader
with some other assignment, or in meeting some other area of
church or community need. Those who have accepted leadership roles are helping the Sunday school team enlarge its influence and effectiveness.

The leadership team is committed to each other as friends
and colaborers through love and deep respect for their leadership skills. They are willing to hold each other accountable by
having different methods of communication streams via one-
to-one conversations, webcasting, regular group meetings, and
training. The team takes joy in working together because they

know what is expected of them and how they fit into God's plan for their church's Sunday school ministry.

To emphasize the value of leadership they have discontinued "workers' meetings" and have implemented "leadership team meetings." The name change has tangibly elevated significance, vision, and appreciation of the Sunday school strategy. The Sunday school teachers, care group leaders, and outreach leaders are beginning to see their roles in the larger scheme of God's kingdom, plan, and work.

The team has become so focused on doing Sunday school the right way that they are committed to helping each and every Sunday school leader to be on the same page. A new focus on modeling spiritual leadership has become contagious. A greater expectation now permeates the Sunday school that involves more leaders, more members, and sets the stage for spiritual transformation.

Does your church have such a leadership team? Do you meet with your Sunday school teachers on a regular basis to inspire, equip, and communicate? The "Great Expectations Leadership Team," as Dunkirk's team is called, helps the congregation understand the purpose of what they are doing not only by equipping but also by telling the stories of transformed lives. They measure their effectiveness by telling the stories. For example, four weeks were recently devoted to telling the stories of God changing lives through the ministry of their Sunday school. Individuals were enlisted and trained in sharing their personal testimonies creatively and uniquely. God moved through that process, and now Sunday school is becoming the foundational place where lives are being changed, and leaders are being developed for service of the Lord.

Finally, they are committed to celebrating what God is doing. It has been said that people own what they create. Here is another way to think about that idea: People celebrate what they own as well. I have seen such a change in the church staff and Sunday school leaders. The former status quo has given birth to a new reality. Dunkirk Baptist Church is seeing and acknowledging a fresh vision of how God can really use their abilities to be a part of God's plan to reach their community for Jesus Christ. A renewed passion for the Sunday school ministry has created the climate for celebration in worship and in their small group gatherings. Leadership is making a difference.

Dunkirk's staff and Sunday school leadership team is overcoming a vacuum of leadership and have defined their effectiveness in the following ways:

- By praying intentionally for specific requests that will help them be effective in having a seven-day-a-week ministry called Sunday school

- By setting up a criteria and a process of what they are looking for in a leader (in other words, they have a very clear picture of the kind of leader they are looking for)

- By adopting a new and fresh leadership development mentality around three words—training, training, training

- By expecting great things including influence, creativity, and results through their leaders

- By adopting "Great Expectations Leadership Team" as their team name to help communicate and model their intentions

- By clearly communicating the vision consistently and telling stories of transformed lives

- By implementing systems and process collaboration to effectively change their Sunday school to be the vehicle for equipping leaders

- By having and expecting a contagious spirit through their leaders in the church

The results are amazing in that other organizations in the church have taken notice and have begun to make changes in how they do ministry more effectively and efficiently.

There are at least five keys for a church in similar circumstances to consider in excelling in equipping leaders.

1. Make sure existing leaders and staff are modeling spiritual leadership, including an intentional lifestyle of prayer.

2. Create a disciplemaking process that can be clearly articulated by the leadership core.

3. Communicate an expectation that most of your membership will be involved in Sunday school and/or small groups.

4. Develop a clear system whereby new members and guests can be plugged into ministry opportunities.

5. Be willing to evaluate your Sunday school ministry to make sure it is assimilating and producing leaders and adjust accordingly.

The principles and value of equipping are not isolated to one church in one type of community. Ephesians 4:11–12 exhorts church leaders in "equipping of the saints for the work of ministry." Equipping is not a regional, cultural, geographically, isolated strategy. It is based on a biblical admonition and is the primary determining factor in the growth of a Sunday school ministry. Here are five other churches that have experienced similar results when excelling in equipping that are located in various regions of North America:

- Richmond Hill Baptist Church, Calgary, Canada
- Cross Lanes Baptist Church, Cross Lanes, WV
- Ogletown Baptist Church, Newark, DE
- Northside Baptist Church, Liverpool, NY
- Island Pond Baptist Church, Hampstead, NH

Please prayerfully consider these questions as you seek to excel in equipping leaders.

- How are you demonstrating a dependence on God?

- What are you believing God for in your ministry of developing leaders?

- Do you have any control issues that you are willing to give to the Lord?

- What is the process for developing leaders in your church? Can your church articulate that process?

- What kind of leader do you desire for your church?

- How are you helping your current leaders to be unified with the mission and vision of your church?

- What steps are you going to take in creating a leadership, mission culture in your church?

The result is that Dunkirk Baptist Church's Sunday school is going through a radical change by moving intentionally away from a one-hour-a-week Bible study to a seven-day-a-week ministry by equipping their leaders, expecting great things, and trusting God for the results. This new era in their church is affecting other organizations and ministries in the church as well. It has not been easy, and has been at times very difficult. However, they are on the right track because it is working. Equipping makes a difference. Seek to excel in equipping in order to help your Sunday school thrive as the members become a blessing to your congregation and your community.

# CHAPTER 9

# Excels with a Volunteer Sunday School Director

## J. D. "Sonny" Tucker

I WAS SHOCKED WHEN THE man walked into the room. I expected a man close to the height of Goliath, the shoulder width of Arnold Schwarzenegger, and the ability to leap tall buildings in a single bound, yet when I finally came face to face with the man hailed as one of the state's best volunteer Sunday school directors—he looked *normal*! Though Bill McCall, volunteer Sunday school director for New Life Baptist Church in Alexander, Arkansas, is indeed a uniquely gifted and special person, he gives hope that "normal" people can do a fantastic job as a volunteer Sunday school director!

Can a Sunday school ministry really excel in the absence of a paid staff member leading the educational ministry? A volunteer Sunday school director may be defined as someone who serves in that capacity as a unpaid/nonprofessional staff member who volunteers for the congregation. That carries two caveats: (1) the congregation relates to and views this person as a non-professional clergy, and (2) this person has another job or career that places high demands on his or her time.

The need for high-quality Sunday school directors who can serve in a volunteer capacity cannot be overstated, due to the tremendous number of churches whose budgets do not allow for a full-time minister of education. The majority of volunteer Sunday school directors function in churches with dual career pastors and staff, or only one full-time pastor, due to budget limitations. Most of these volunteer leaders must serve without a formal degree in church education. The result is that many churches settle for a warm body to fill this position who may do no more than turn on the coffee pot on Sunday morning and occasionally order literature. A vast majority of churches either have a single staff or bivocational pastor with no additional paid ministerial staff. Demands on the pastor's time require that some of the delegation of the vital ministry of small groups be assigned to a volunteer. While the pastor plays a key leadership role and cannot effectively delegate the whole of the education ministry to another leader, he or she must enlist and work side by side with someone to assist with the details of the strategy. The health of the church can be seriously impacted if the pastor fails to understand the role or if the volunteer is not equipped for his or her task in leading the Sunday school ministry. Thus, the great need for thousands of volunteer Sunday school directors who can serve with knowledge, tools, commitment, and skill.

## NEW LIFE BAPTIST CHURCH, ALEXANDER, ARKANSAS

The church sits on the southwest side of Little Rock. The pastor, Dr. James Sidney "Sid" Sample, is one of those guys who can't seem to stay retired and was blessed to cease aging once he turned sixty. He says he is in his late seventies, but that is difficult to believe given his and Mrs. Sample's energy, vitality, youthfulness, and passion for life and ministry. When Sid became the pastor of New Life Church in October of 2008, the church was averaging ninety-nine in Sunday school attendance; they saw the average double within four years. The church is located in a neighborhood sitting on the edge of rural Arkansas and a Little Rock bedroom community. The growth of New Life Church underscores the fact that churches with volunteer Sunday school directors can provide a top quality Sunday school ministry.

## THE PASTOR'S ROLE

It is immediately evident that the pastor plays a vital role in the Sunday school ministry at New Life. There exists a strong kingdom partnership between pastor and Sunday school director, and this connection and pastoral support is immediately evident. Bill McCall says that the pastor has set the vision for the church and the Sunday school. The Sunday school director is a partner committed to help fulfill that vision.

McCall has identified five critical leadership factors employed by Pastor Sid in leading the church to prioritize Sunday school. First, the pastor truly believes in the vital importance of Sunday school in the life of the church. Pastor Sid knows that when people are mere attendees of the worship service, they may not really have a sense of belonging or connection to that particular congregation. However, those who only attend worship do have a sense of connection to the pastor. This leaves the church in a weakened state because it is built around the pastor's pulpit ministry, personality, and personal ministry. When people are connected to a small group, as well as the pastor, the church is much healthier. A connection to a small group like Sunday school ensures that the participant is connected in the absence of the pastor or in the circumstance where the pastor leaves the church whether through calling or because of crisis.

Secondly, the pastor promotes the Sunday school from the pulpit. The member in the pew will ordinarily focus on those things to which the pastor gives priority. Thirdly, the pastor directly supports the work of the Sunday school and the Sunday school director. Pastor Sid is involved in every aspect of the Sunday school, not only in word but also in his actions. Pastor Sid attends training, visits the classes, and actively invites people to Sunday school.

Another facet of Pastor Sid's support of Sunday school is that he gives the Sunday school organization and the Sunday school director the freedom to try new strategies, methods, programs, etc. If the plan is well thought out and prayed over, then Sid supports the new strategy. And lastly, not only does the pastor give the Sunday school organization and the Sunday school director the freedom to try new things, but he also gives the freedom to fail. Providing for an occasional failure is not an excuse for laziness, poor planning, or haphazard execution. It is understanding that not everything will truly work. But the freedom to try and fail at new strategies and methods opens the door for discovery of new ministry venues that take a church to the next level.

## QUALITIES OF AN EFFECTIVE VOLUNTEER SUNDAY SCHOOL DIRECTOR

Pastor Sid states that it is "vital that a church have a high quality and committed leader to serve as a Sunday school director, and Bill McCall is that type of a person." He feels most Sunday school directors see their role as merely "a position to fill and a program to glibly run. Bill's commitment to his role as Sunday school director is in massive contradistinction to that mind-set."

Pastor Sid recounts the qualities that he identified in Bill McCall that caused him to pursue Bill as his partner in building a strong Sunday school. Three traits were obvious in Bill. First, he possesses a great passion for spiritual matters. Bill's priority of having an active and dedicated walk with Christ affects every aspect of his life, including his church, his position as volunteer

Sunday school director, and his gracious and kind treatment of people.

The second trait that drew Pastor Sid to enlist Bill McCall as Sunday school director was that he is a committed and dependable leader. Bill McCall does what leaders are supposed to do. He is committed to being fruitful and effective in his work. He strives to learn the position and gives attention to details that pertain to it. He arrives to church focused and prepared to do his job. He is punctual in his responsibilities and duties. He is dependable in every aspect of his relationship to his church.

The third characteristic that stands out in Bill McCall is that the members at New Life Church follow Bill in his leadership position as Sunday school director. The congregation has gifted Bill with "followship." The church views their director as a key leader due to his commitment and love for the church and its work. The Sunday school teachers and officers respect him because he is a servant and does all within his means to assist and undergird them. Because he is gracious, kind, and winsome in his dealings with them, they are motivated to partner with him in building a great, small group ministry.

## COMPONENTS OF EXCELLING WITH A VOLUNTEER DIRECTOR

Bill McCall identifies six areas of focus in fulfilling his role as volunteer Sunday school director for New Life Church. First, the Sunday school teachers must be supported and deeply valued. He knows them personally, and they know him. He is accessible and is there to serve them. The teachers are keenly aware that the entire congregation places great value on Sunday school teachers, and that by serving as a teacher they are performing a very vital ministry to the Lord. Bill is visible each Sunday greeting teachers and classes, expressing encouragement, and affirmation.

The second factor in their success in Sunday school is the quarterly teacher's meeting. This is a high-octane, high energy meeting that maximizes time and meets needs. Bill describes these meetings as a "huddle" or "pep talk" used to encourage, motivate, and express appreciation to teachers. He also listens to their challenges, and they discuss ways to overcome them. Success stories are celebrated and detailed. Ideas are traded on how the classes conduct effective follow-up and fellowship. "Training bytes" are an important component of these meetings. Bill ensures that basic leadership skills are covered concerning lesson plans, class dynamics, and the relational aspects of Sunday school.

The third component of the Sunday school success at New Life Church is the emphasis on guest ministry. This aspect of small group ministry is underscored by both director and pastor as being an absolute top priority. Making guests feel welcome, affirmed, valued, and important is a source of constant training and emphasis. Pastor Sid and Bill both are actively involved in the guest ministry and set a fantastic example for the Sunday school and congregation to follow. Teachers are expected to arrive early and be there to personally greet each guest. Hosts and hostesses, armed with name tags, personally escort each first-time guest from the welcome center to the Sunday school class. Guests are greeted by teachers and class members where they enjoy fellowship and light refreshments. Pastor and Sunday school director alike strive to make it extremely difficult to attend New Life as a guest without being made to feel like one is valued by God and the members of his church. Bill believes you have to offer attendees what they can't get by watching a worship service on television—personal interaction with people who truly care about you and deeply desire to engage you in their friendship group.

A fourth element of New Life's Sunday school is that the volunteer Sunday school director applies good organizational skills. Curriculum and resources are ordered on time and placed in the classrooms in a timely manner. The Sunday school secretary maintains proper records. Guest and prospect information is up to date and thorough. The absence of haphazard management and organization instills a sense of pride in the Sunday school ministry from the teacher's and officer's perspective, and signals to them that they are valued and are devoting their time to a very worthwhile cause.

A fifth component of the Sunday school organization is the enlistment of teachers and workers. Though the Sunday school personnel are channeled through the nominating committee for final approval, the Sunday school director and pastor have a major leadership role in this process. When it comes to teachers of new classes, they are hand-selected by the pastor and Sunday school director. Pastor Sid and Bill are constantly in search of emerging leaders in the church. They understand that a key component of strategic church leadership is identifying, enlisting, training, deploying, and supporting Sunday school teachers. The value they place on the Sunday school in general and new classes in particular drive them to place the absolute best leaders in these positions.

The last, and one of the most important components of New Life's effective Sunday school organization, is their intentionality in starting new small groups. Bill, Pastor Sid, and the entire church understand the necessity of beginning new classes to reach new people. Creating new groups is a continual focus and priority for New Life Church. Pastor Sid writes a letter to all potential new Sunday school members inviting them to be a part of the small group ministry, especially when new classes are forming. New Life Church builds their new classes on specialty groups or target groups, especially those with unique ministry needs. These may include singles, singles again, ladies whose husbands do not attend church, and young married couples. They can prove anecdotally that the rule found in any standard Sunday school manual is true—for every class you start and conduct properly will result in a gain of ten in average Sunday school attendance.

## THE SUM OF THE MATTER

It may be suggested that the major applications from New Life Church in Alexander, Arkansas for churches with volunteer Sunday school directors may be summarized by three keys. First, churches should do everything related to Sunday school with excellence. One of the great keys of leadership is to know what really is worth priority, attention, time, and effort and what is not. Time, budgets, manpower, and focus are limited and must be channeled to ministry venues worthy of priority. New Life would say the Sunday school work and ministry is top priority for a commitment to excellence.

The second key from New Life is the priority of an effective ministry to welcome guests. A church possesses only one chance to make a great first impression. The initial and secondary steps in ministry to guests must be extremely effective in connecting the guest to the small group.

The third key is the importance of beginning new small groups for new people. New members bond quicker in newly formed groups and are more effectively assimilated into the life of the church through the vehicle of new classes.

These three commitments have proven to be very effective in driving New Life Church to having a high impact with the leadership of a key volunteer. Bill McCall is proof that you can be a dynamic volunteer Sunday school director even if you are not able to leap over tall buildings in a single bound.

# CHAPTER 10

# Excels with an Attendance Campaign

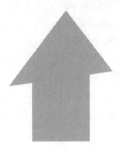

## *Elmer Towns*

FRIEND DAY IS AN ATTENDANCE campaign that became a national movement when a young lady—Kathy Burley—was reached for Jesus Christ through Heritage Baptist Church in Forest, Virginia. At the time, Heritage was a church plant averaging about sixty people in a store front building in a strip mall. I was asked to speak at the first service of Heritage Baptist Church in its new but small auditorium, approximately one mile away.[1]

This Friend Day outreach program came at a great time for this young church because of (1) Intentional Evangelism.[2] Pastor

---

1.  I counseled Rodney Kidd how to have a *Friend Day*, so he invited me to preach the sermon that day. It was so successful that I told the story all over America. Because many pastors wanted to have a *Friend Day*, I wrote a *Friend Day* resource packet with Larry Gilbert, president of Church Growth Institute. You can order the resource packet from http://store.churchgrowth.org/epages/ChurchGrowth.sf or 1-800-553-GROW (4769).
2.  *Intentional Evangelism* is when a believer prays for a specific friend, relative, associate, or neighbor to become a Christian. Then the believer makes specific plans to influence their unsaved friend to become a Christian.

Rodney Kidd planned to reach the lost friends of his members when they moved into their new building. (2) Accountability Evangelism.[3] Kidd asked everyone to invite a neighbor to the new building and get their friend to promise attendance by filling out a "Yes" card. Their signature and "Yes" indicated they would be present. Then, Pastor Kidd had each member hold up their card before the congregation. The fact "Yes" cards were shown publicly indicated how each person fulfilled their responsibility.

When I told my wife Ruth the plans, she said, "Get me a "Yes" card; I have someone I want to bring with me." My wife didn't want me to be embarrassed because she wasn't bringing an unsaved friend. Ruth and Kathy Burley shared a realtor's office and had many conversations about salvation. Kathy was an honest seeker and had attended several kinds of churches searching for God, i.e., Roman Catholic, Pentecostal, Presbyterian. Now this was her chance to attend a Baptist church.

The people responded so enthusiastically to the Friend Day campaign that a total of seventy-seven "Yes" cards were gathered. Then Kidd asked me, "Can I expect 154 people to come on Friend Day (seventy-seven visitors and seventy-seven members)?" I answered his question with a question. "Would you be happy if one hundred people came?" The church had never gone over one hundred in attendance.

"Absolutely!" Rod answered. "I'd be happy if only one visitor came."

Friend Day was a rousing success—236 people attended the church. The new pews were filled to capacity, folding chairs had to be set up, and still people stood around the edges of the morning crowd.

Statistics from Friend Day campaigns indicate most people do not make a decision the first time they visit a church; rather,

---

3.  *Accountability Evangelism* is when a believer takes responsibility for an unsaved person and does all he/she can do to bring them to Christ.

they have to visit the church about three times before making a meaningful decision to join or to trust Jesus as Savior. (3) The Law of 3 Hearings. I preached the sermon, and at the invitation no one came forward.

Rodney Kidd had planned a comprehensive follow-up campaign to contact each guest seven times. (4) The Law of Seven Touches.[4] Each of those who visited received a letter every three or four days: the first letter thanking them for their attendance, the second letter explaining the ministries of the church, the third letter detailed coming activities at the church, and the fourth letter contained general advertisement. While the letters were being sent every other day, different visitation teams went out to make personal contacts with all the Friend Day guests.

Mike, Kathy Burley's husband noted, "We didn't have any friends in Lynchburg before we went to Heritage Church." Then he went on to explain that every couple of days they got a personal letter from someone in the church. Then in the evenings a knock would come at the door around 7 p.m. Mike would say, "That's someone from the church; we don't know anyone else in this town." Then he joked, "We haven't been lonely since we visited Heritage Baptist Church."

Two weeks after Friend Day, Rod Kidd phoned me around 9:30 one evening to tell me, "Kathy and Mike Burley just prayed to receive Christ this evening." Kidd had visited them that evening. Their hearts were prepared for conversation by the friendliness of the church to trust Jesus Christ as Savior and Lord.

## FRIEND DAY WORKS IN LARGER CHURCHES

Jonathan Falwell, pastor of Thomas Road Baptist Church,

---

4.  Statistics reveal a person makes a positive response to the gospel after there have been seven or eight meaningful encounters with the gospel, or with those who are trying to win them to Christ. Statistics found in Flavil R. Yeakley, "Persuasion in Religious Conversion" (Doctoral Dissertation, University of Illinois, 1975).

Lynchburg, Virginia, said, "As a young man growing up in this church, I repeatedly saw the positive effects of a 'Friend Day' used by my father, Jerry Falwell. Many were brought into the church. I fully support the new title, 'My Friendship Connection.'" In 2008, Jonathan Falwell led the church to have one of the greatest Friend Day events ever. There were over twelve thousand in attendance with 2,676 "Friends," and fifty-one salvation decisions. Jonathan asked the congregation to place an "X" on the visitor's card if anyone wanted him to call and explain more about going to heaven.

## FRIEND DAY WORKS IN SMALLER CHURCHES

Pastor Terry Mosley of Temple Free Will Baptist Church in Greenville, North Carolina said his church's average attendance was 190 to 200, but they had 370 in attendance on Friend Day, and thirteen people trusted Jesus as their Savior. Mosley exclaimed, "What a service! Our attendance was up almost fifty percent and before our follow-up visitation, we had a twenty-three-year-old lady saved as well. Needless to say, our people are more excited than ever."[5]

Friend Day can be one of the most successful events on the church calendar to bring unchurched people into the church, but it is not just a "slogan"—nor does it work just because church leaders are announcing that everyone should bring a friend on a specific Sunday. It's an interactive strategy that involves everyone, and, in so doing, it teaches church members new skills in (5) Relationship Evangelism,[6] so that they reach their friends, relatives, associates, and neighbors all on the same Sunday.

Friend Day can function like a revival for a church but is a

---

5.   Pastor Terry Mosley used *My Friendship Connection*, available from http://myfriendshipconnection.com/home. For more information, call Vernon Brady, 434-528-6549.

6.   Using existing relationships to influence a person to Christ so that they make a meaningful decision for salvation.

completely different strategy of outreach. The traditional revival is geared to the spiritual ability of the evangelist to attract the crowd, present the gospel, and actually win people to Jesus Christ. Friend Day does not focus on a visiting evangelist, rather it focuses on each member leveraging their relationship to win their friends to Jesus Christ. Week-long evangelistic events such as revivals can reach people for Christ but can be limited because:

- Often both husband and wife work, so they have less time to attend church.

- Schedules of children have become increasingly complex.

- The pervasiveness of television and other forms of entertainment interfere.

- The number of church evangelists has declined.

- Negative images toward church evangelists hinder attendance.

Research shows that approximately eighty-six percent of all who are converted to Christ do so through the influence of a family or friend. This is called *Relationship Evangelism* or *Friendship Evangelism*. Therefore, Friend Day is a campaign that takes advantage of this research to help Christians in local churches become "spiritual influences" to reach their friends and to bring them to church where they will hear the gospel and become Christians.

Johnny Hunt, pastor of First Baptist Church, Woodstock, Georgia, past president of the Southern Baptist Convention wanted to find out what brought the people of First Woodstock to Christ. Knowing precisely how they came to Christ would help him prepare a strategy to be more effective to reach more. Several thousand were present the Sunday night he did a simple "hand raise" survey. "How many were primarily motivated to receive Christ because of something like a tract, billboard, door hanger, or TV?" Less than ten people raised a hand. "How many came to Christ because of a pastoral contact?" Again, less than ten hands were raised. "How many were reached through our visitation program?" Again, less than ten hands were raised. "How many came because of the simple invitation of a friend or relative?" A powerful picture was seen as thousands in the room lifted their hand to show *relationship evangelism* is the most effective outreach in our contemporary society. There was no question. Johnny Hunt, and everyone present, knew exactly what they needed to do to be most effective in reaching more for Christ. Friends must reach their friends for Christ.

Rick Rasberry surveyed five thousand churches from a list of those that recently had purchased Friend Day resources. In his doctrinal dissertation, Rasberry demonstrated that churches were successful when they carefully followed the directions of the packet and got the following results:

- Churches added fourteen percent of their first-time visitors to the church membership.

- Churches had an average of six decisions on the actual Friend Day with eleven decisions made for Christ during the four-week follow-up campaign.

- Church attendance increased six percent.

- Churches sustained their growth over the average attendance for the previous year.[7]

---

7.   Rick L. Rasberry, "An Analysis of the *Friend Day* Program, Written by Elmer Towns and Published by Church Growth Institute" (Doctoral Dissertation, Liberty Baptist Theological Seminary, 1995).

Phil Campbell is a small town in Northwest Alabama. The census of 2000 identified only 1,091 people residing in the town. There are nine churches located there and many would think the town is too small and has too many churches to have a greater impact for the kingdom. However, Pastor Sammy Taylor of Mountainview Baptist Church learned differently as he led his people to pray for Friend Day. Pastor Taylor reported, "I haven't seen this much excitement in our church in years. The two crosses in the sanctuary are loaded down with "Yes" connect cards.[8] There were a total of 187 souls (cards) that need to be touched by Jesus. Because of Friend Day, eight people trusted Christ, and about twenty-five "unchurched" are still attending. Because of continued follow-up, Pastor Taylor baptized thirty-eight people that year. Taylor was excited to report, "Our second attempt at Friend Day was even better than the first."

On Wednesday, April 27, 2011 powerful EF-5 tornadoes with winds in excess of 210 miles per hour ripped through the small town, and most of the community was destroyed including Mountainview Baptist Church. The church buildings were leveled, leaving only the parking lot and lots of memories. Many of the survivors showed up on the asphalt parking lot for a sermon by Pastor Sammy Taylor for a word of hope and to bury the dead. On each previous Friend Day, Taylor had carefully informed the people "If you ever need a pastor to talk with you or pray with you, please call me." This clearly was the time that Pastor Taylor was recognized as the leader because of all the friendship connections his church had made in the community on Friend Day.

---

8. The church used *My Friendship Connection*, an updated form of *Friend Day*, available at http://www.myfriendshipconnection.com. This plan calls the "Yes" cards, "Connect cards." It suggests the cards with names of friends be attached to a cross in the sanctuary.

## STEPS FOR FRIEND DAY

During the four weeks before Friend Day, the church should begin gathering names and addresses of those who have been invited to attend on Friend Day and those that promised they will attend Friend Day. These prospects would then receive a daily contact (through email or regular mail) on the theme of "Becoming a Friend of God." (This is a daily thought designed to bring the reader to know Jesus Christ as their friend. It is also a daily devotional for church members to learn their obligations to reach prospects, how to motivate them, and how to use their friendship to bring them to church.) Every day new items of events on Friend Day will be included in the email to keep announcements fresh, sparkling, so people will anticipate finding out new things when they actually come on Friend Day.

## WEEKLY STRATEGY

**Week One:** Pastor preaches a sermon on the theme of "Let's Celebrate Our Friends." In this sermon, he sets the vision for relationship evangelism. This first sermon is key to all that follows because the First Law of Leadership is applied, "when the people buy into the pastor's vision, they buy into his leadership." Therefore, it is imperative that the congregation accepts the pastor's vision of "*each one* be a friend, so that *each one* can win a friend to Christ."

*Pastor introduces inviting campaign.* The pastor and/or the campaign manager will hold up a letter from a friend in the Week One morning church service and read it to the congregation, indicating their friend will attend Friend Day as their friend. Then the pastor will post a "Yes" card from his friend on a cross in the front of the auditorium.

All adult and youth Sunday school teachers will present a Bible study on "Relationship Evangelism." This lesson will have different content from the pulpit sermon, but will reinforce the theme of relationship evangelism.

*Daily Bible reading.* The church will print in its bulletin a daily Bible reading that leads up to a celebration of friendship. Each daily Bible reading comes out of the daily devotional book, *Becoming a Friend for God.*

*Daily devotional.* Members will be encouraged to purchase the book, or the church will purchase and distribute daily insights on *Becoming a Friend for God.* The last section of each devotional called "Your Assignment" will include daily practical activities that focus on bringing a friend to church so that the friend can be won to Christ. Reader assignments over the following four weeks involve making a prayer list, praying with another, writing up a testimony, making a phone call, and following through on different activities for each of the four weeks leading up to Friend Day.

Churches will purchase a disc with the four weeks of devotionals that will be e-mailed to every member of the congregation every day. This e-mail will constantly involve every member in their responsibility of reaching their friends for Christ.

**Week Two:** Pastor will preach a sermon on the theme of, "It's Imperative to have Friends," and the Sunday school teachers will present the theme, "Why God Gave You Friends."

*Church board invitation campaign.* Each church board member (Deacons, Elders, Key Congregational Leaders) will be given an opportunity during the morning service to tell the church whom their friend will be on Friend Day. Letters written to board members will be posted on a cross at the front of the church auditorium to give credibility and accountability to the congregation.

**Week Three:** Pastor will preach a sermon on the theme of "A Community of Friends," which is a sermon to emphasize that the local church must not only be a community of believers, but also its members must incorporate their unchurched friends into fellowship with the body to be influenced by God, so they can respond to the gospel.

The emphasis is that we must extend pastoral care to every friend of all members to show them the love of Jesus and to help them come to know Christ.

The Sunday school teacher will follow the same theme with the lesson, "You Can't Live Without Friends."

*Sunday school leader inviting campaign.* Each Sunday school teacher will show their "Yes" card to the congregation and post the card on the cross at the front of the church auditorium. Each teacher will be given an opportunity during the morning service to tell the name of their friend they are bringing on Friend Day. This public announcement gives credibility to Friend Day.

**Week Four:** The pastor will preach a sermon on the theme of, "God Loves Celebrations." This will point out that God always had celebrations in the Old Testament, i.e., Passover, Firstfruits, Pentecost, etc. Each of these are centered around a meal, fellowship, and renewing relationship with one another. This sermon creates excitement for celebrating Friend Day the following week.

The Sunday school class will teach a lesson on "We Need One Another," pointing out that no man can live without friends, and that the church is one of the greatest places to find friends.

*"Every member" campaign.* Each member will be given an opportunity during the morning service to post their "Yes" cards on the cross for all to see.

Use the week before Friend Day for an all-out endeavor to get friends to attend who have previously signed a "Yes" card. This is a concentrated outreach to everyone who has said they will attend Friend Day to remind them of the time, place, and latest announcements of exciting things that will happen on Friend Day.

**Week Five:** On Friend Day, some churches will invite a guest speaker; however, it's best for the pastor to preach even when he is not a strong speaker. Why? Because potential members make their decision to connect to a church based on their relationship and perception of the local pastor.

The theme of the pastor's sermon: "God Has a Wonderful Plan for His Friends."

The Sunday school classes that week should emphasize testimonies rather than a Bible study for this Sunday. The class meeting will be organized around relationships, including refreshments and fellowship activities. Some Christians should share their testimony of how they came to Christ through the influence of a friend or family.

**Weeks Six Through Eight:** The success of Friend Day is the continued relationship between the church member and guest who attended with them.

After a Friend Day, the church will organize a three-fold campaign to follow up all guests. An invitation campaign will contact visitors each day with a devotional to establish a relationship between the visitor and God. The second strategy is a personal contact between the friend and church member (visit, meal or coffee together, phone call). The third strategy is an advertising campaign to advise the visitor of coming events at the church.

Over fifty thousand churches have used the old Friend Day resource packet. Why do churches continue to use Friend Day?

Because friendship is timeless and can be effective at any time, in any community, and resonates with every generation. The idea of Christians having friends is transcendent, and Christians have always wanted some practical help in influencing their friends to know Jesus Christ as Savior.

Friend Day is a local church driven campaign that motivates members to invite their friends to church for a special celebration of friendship on a Sunday morning. Enthusiasm generated by relationships will drive Sunday morning excitement. Adding to the excitement will be notable guests such as local politicians, special music, activities on the lawn for children, refreshment tables throughout the church, special decorations and banners, plus a focus on friendship and our relationships.

## CONCLUSION

God has put each believer within a local community of people—the Church—and the Bible teaches this is the body of Christ. This local community gets its marching orders from the Bible. The word *together* is the spiritual basis for fellowship among Christians as they fellowship with Christ. However, the ultimate expression of fellowship is when each believer extends *relationship evangelism* to their friends and family to incorporate them into the local community of believers, the church.

God never intended you to fulfill your purpose in life alone. As a matter of fact, you can't find the plan of God for your life apart from others. Therefore, you find the plan of God for your life in community, and this ultimately touches your friends.

Every local church is commanded to carry out the Great Commission. Since the church is commanded to evangelize all, this includes friends and relatives. Therefore, *friendship evangelism* must be a part of your church to reach out, and specifically, your church reaches out through *relationship evangelism*.

The following resources can help your congregation implement an attendance campaign that can help your Sunday school to excel:

## RESOURCES

### *FRIEND DAY RESOURCE PACKET:*

Ephesians Four Ministries
Church Growth Institute
1-800-553-GROW (4769)
Friend Day Supplies: Everything you need to plan and carry out the nation's most popular attendance campaign!
See http://store.churchgrowth.org/epages/churchgrowth. sf/4e8b2c670144fb5e2717ac1003570620/catalog/1012/1

### *MY FRIENDSHIP CONNECTION:*

My Friendship Connection is a five week outreach campaign designed to engage members of your church in a strategy of intentionally inviting friends and reaching them for Jesus Christ. By joining with us, you will leverage years of expertise and critical learning from leaders like: Dr. Elmer Towns, Dr. Johnny Hunt, Dr. Bobby Welch, Dr. James Merritt, Dr. Mac Brunson, Dr. Frank Page, Greg Stier (Dare2Share Ministry) and many others.

> "Yes, people are still open to spiritual conversations. Vernon Brady and Elmer Towns provide a new tool to help start those conversations. My Friendship Connection is a great tool to help churches involve their people in reaching their community for Christ." —Ed Stetzer, Director, LifeWay Research

See http://myfriendshipconnection.com

# CHAPTER 11

# Excels Out of Decline

## *Bob Mayfield*

INOLA, OKLAHOMA IS A SMALL town with a population of 1,788 people located about twenty miles east of Tulsa. Known as the "Hay Capital of the World," Inola is also home to a church that excels in doing the basics of Sunday school. Although the church's Sunday school is on the rise, it had not always been that way. Like many churches, First Baptist had lost its focus: its focus on evangelism, its focus on discipleship, and its focus on Sunday school. The church's best days appeared to be behind it. Church members, though faithful, were discouraged. Due to some inner church conflicts, the trust of the people in one another (and in the future of the church) was broken. But with the calling of a new pastor and renewed zeal for evangelism and discipleship, things began to turn around.

During the interview I had with the pastor and the leaders of the church's Sunday school, one could almost feel the enthusiasm and energy in the room. These people are mobilized and motivated to give leadership and direction to a new course of action for their church and their Sunday school.

## THE ROLE OF THE PASTOR

Church members tend to prioritize those things that are important to their pastor. Pastor Blake Gideon is a passionate man. He is passionate about Jesus Christ, reaching people with the gospel, and organizing the church through Sunday school. A former oil-field worker, Gideon committed his life to Jesus as Lord while in his early twenties and soon accepted the call into full time vocational ministry. He went on to earn a bachelor's degree and later received two master degrees from Southwestern Seminary, one in Christian education and the other degree in theology. Gideon's enthusiasm to reach people with the gospel is authentic and contagious.

Arriving in Inola after two previous pastorates where he also turned around declining churches, Gideon went straight to work. Rather than making broad sweeping announcements of change from the pulpit, he enlisted a "Sunday School Council" to help implement the changes needed to bring an evangelistic focus to the church's Sunday school. Gideon sees the pastor's role in the Sunday school in the following ways. First, the pastor must be the champion of the Sunday school. Like many pastors of growing Sunday schools, if a person only has time during the week to attend either Sunday school or the worship service, Gideon encourages his congregation to attend Sunday school. Through the Sunday morning groups, a person receives the Bible study, ministry, prayer, and personal relationships that are so critical.

Secondly, the pastor must cast a consistent vision. In many churches, the members do not have a compelling vision of the Sunday school. If left on their own, these members will often recast a vision that meets their own preferences. The difficulty in casting vision, especially in plateaued and declining churches, cannot be underestimated. Through the years, many leaders in the church can become complacent about the direction of the congregation. This attitude often leads to mediocrity, the total opposite of an excelling Sunday school.

Casting a consistent vision is vital if the Sunday school is to excel. Gideon's strategy as pastor and vision-caster is to communicate a consistent, solid message about the purpose of Sunday school to the members and leaders. Inola does not chase fads or make constant, sweeping changes about its vision. Pastor Gideon is consistent in promoting Sunday school as the primary strategy for evangelism, discipleship, and ministry.

The pastor is not only the champion of the church's Sunday school and its vision-caster, but he is also the team leader. Early in his tenure at the church, Pastor Gideon wrote the church's Sunday school vision. The vision outlines the church's purpose behind having Sunday school, how the ministry will be led, the expectations of the organization in general. The vision also outlines the leadership as well as provides job descriptions for each ministry position in the church. Gideon printed his vision for Sunday school and distributed it to every member of the church so that everyone knew his plans and heart for a Sunday school of excellence that would impact not only the town of Inola but also engage the church in missions through the Sunday school ministry.

Gideon writes:

> When we are faithful to live our lives in obedience to God, seeking to glorify Him, excellence is the result. I believe if we "do not merely look out for your (our) own personal interests, but also for the interests of others" (Philippians 2:4) by praying for the lost, ministering to the lost, and sharing the gospel with the lost, we are following the example set forth by the early church in the book of Acts. My desire is to see every Sunday school class and/or department build upon this vision by implementing prayer coordinators and teams, ministry coordinators and teams, and evangelism coordinators and teams. I have a vision of seeing missions and church planting becoming a part of the DNA of our church family.

However, in order for this to happen, it first must become part of the DNA of our Sunday school.

Implementing a Vision for Change, Gideon enlisted a Sunday school team. Composed of ten people plus the pastor, Gideon empowered the team to join him in developing a strategy to implement his vision for the church's Sunday school. The team is made up of the education director, the director of each age group division (preschool, children, student, and adults), the church's outreach director, prayer director, and ministry director. This team met with Gideon over several months to develop the church's strategy for Sunday school. Notice how the structure of the team mirrors the vision cast by the pastor. In addition to the age-group directors, there is a director each for prayer, ministry, and outreach. The Sunday school team met weekly to develop a strategy to implement the pastor's vision. They developed a simple, accountable strategy to implement Gideon's vision through the entire organization.

In addition to the department director and the teacher, every class is organized around three teams whose purposes are to pray, minister, and reach out to the lost in the community. Three people from the class are enlisted to provide leadership and enlist a team of people to help them with their assigned task. Each group is held accountable to implement the strategy set forth by Gideon and the Sunday school team. Implementing the strategy is not just a suggestion, but an expectation. Every class is expected to submit the names of their prayer, ministry, and outreach leaders. In addition, they submit names of the people in the class that are ministering on the teams as well.

Implementing the church's Sunday school strategy is actually done through the teams in the individual classes. The vision is not just an empty statement relegated to paper, but it is a strategy that pervades the entire Sunday school ministry. Accountability is vital in order for a Sunday school to excel.

After developing and implementing their strategy, the Sunday school team continues to meet every Wednesday evening throughout the year. At these gatherings, each director gives an update from their area of responsibility. As the implementation of the strategy began to unfold, the church began to adopt what they call a "no flop-down policy." Essentially, the underlying goal of the church's strategy is that no member is allowed to walk in and flop down. Each member is expected to serve on one of the teams. Ultimately, the goal of the Sunday school council is to have every class in the church fully engaged in the church's "Pursuing Excellence" strategy.

## CONNECTING VISION AND STRATEGY

The pastor has cast a vision of excellence regarding Bible study, prayer, ministry, and outreach. The Sunday school council has taken the vision to the next level of developing an overall strategy for the entire Sunday school. Now the next step is taken, and each class is challenged to be fully engaged in implementing the church strategy in their individual groups. A look into Inola's strategy reveals a vital aspect of developing vision and strategy. Churches often have one without the other. A church that is strong on vision, but has not followed through with an adequate strategy, will quickly lose momentum. Vision and enthusiasm can only carry a church family so far. Eventually, some type of strategy must be implemented to see that the vision is being done throughout the organization. Conversely, a congregation that is implementing a strategy without a vision will ultimately find itself pulled in many directions or perhaps moving in the wrong direction. The members lose heart and the strategy, as good as it may look on paper, will grind to a halt because of a lack of vision. Sunday schools that excel must have a healthy combination of vision and strategy if they are to truly excel.

Pastor Gideon invested a full year of preaching and casting a vision for a Sunday school that excels. But just what does an excelling Sunday school look like? In order for people to understand the vision, Gideon cast a mental picture of what the church would look like when they achieved their goal. Gideon's goal was to see people come to faith in Jesus through the Sunday school groups. Sunday school would be a place where evangelism took place.

Furthermore, each class would become the church's primary place of personal care and ministry once a person trusted Jesus as Savior. The design is to ensure that no member would ever go through a crisis alone. Gideon also expressed a vision that "God's house would be a place of prayer." Every member would not only receive ministry but would also be supported by prayer.

Finally, every member would experience life-changing Bible study each week through the church's Sunday school ministry. After receiving this vision from the pastor, the Sunday School council set out to develop and cast the strategy that they would ask each class in the church to adopt. The strategy put the implementation squarely on each class. Each class would, therefore, be accountable for staffing and implementing the strategy. The strategy was developed from Gideon's vision of prayer, ministry, and evangelism.

In summary, the pastor cast the vision and enlisted the Sunday school council. The council developed the strategy and enlisted the support of each class. Each class implemented the strategy and became accountable to the Sunday school team for results.

## EXPECTING THE BEST FROM CLASSES

The strategy at Inola is for every class to have the following leaders: Bible teacher, group coordinator, prayer leader, ministry leader, and outreach leader. The group coordinator's ministry is to organize the class for excellence. He or she takes the responsibility to enlist and oversee the team leaders for each of the class's three ministry functions.

First, each group has a prayer team. The responsibilities of the team are to lead the class to do more than just register prayer requests but to seek ways to meet needs of those mentioned for prayer. Consider these examples of how each class engages prayer.

- **Prayer quads.** Instead of thirty minutes of prayer and prayer requests, at the end of each group meeting the class gets into prayer quads. These groups of four people each then write their requests on an index card and pass the card to their left. Each person then prays for the requests of their neighbor.

- **Evangelism prayer lists.** Classes keep a list of lost or unchurched people that they know personally. These people are lifted up in prayer at every group meeting.

- **Unreached people groups.** Every Sunday school class at Inola has adopted an unreached people group from the denomination's International Mission Board. These groups are prayed for weekly by each class.

- **Prayer walks.** The church is located across the street from a local school. To help engage their children's Sunday school classes, every Wednesday night the children conduct a prayer walk for their school.

Secondly, each class has a ministry team with a leader enlisted and designated. These teams are responsible for both ministry within the class and also missions in the community. Ministry teams receive prayer requests from the prayer team for those who have specific needs that the group can tangibly address in addition to praying. Each ministry team is also expected to lead the class to have three ministry projects throughout the year. These projects are targeted at three areas: an internal (class) project, a church project, and an outreach project.

The focus on an outreach project led the church's ministry leaders to treat the town of Inola like a missionary would engage a mission field. Each class in the church adopted a neighborhood and has remained engaged with it. One result of the neighborhood strategy came as a result of one class roofing a house in its adopted neighborhood. As a result of this ministry, a family from the neighborhood began attending the church, and a family member has become a follower of Jesus Christ. One children's Sunday school class adopted the local nursing home, and the class makes several visits to the nursing facility each year.

Thirdly, every class has an evangelism team leader. The church meets for outreach every Monday night, and it is the responsibility of this team leader to enlist a class representative to participate each week. One key aspect of the evangelism team is that it is the recipient of much of the work of the other two teams. People in need of the gospel that are discovered by the ministry team are shared with the evangelism team. In addition, the first Monday night of each month is evangelistic prayer night. People in need of salvation that church members have identified are prayed for by name. In addition, unchurched guests who have attended church sponsored events like Vacation Bible School or youth camp are also lifted up in prayer.

Pastor Gideon also offers an evangelistic Bible study group in his home every Monday night after churchwide outreach. Often, people who are visited by an evangelism team attend this study in order to learn more about the gospel and as a way to personally connect with the pastor. Members of the evangelism team are encouraged to visit homes in groups of two or three. Many members bring one of their children with them as their visitation partner. These children have been so encouraged by evangelism that many of them lead the prayer time as they get in the car to make visits.

Like any strategy, a vital component of success is follow-through and accountability. Therefore, the church strives for excellence by clearing the calendar for Sunday school leadership meetings. You may recall that the Sunday school Team meets every Wednesday evening. At this meeting, each age division gives a report. This is not necessarily a statistical or numerical report as much as it is a ministry report. Members of the Sunday school council share reports of who in the church is being prayed for, who is being ministered to in their area, and also evangelism reports from Monday night.

## TO DIVE OR TO THRIVE: THAT IS THE QUESTION

Casting a vision, engaging leaders in developing a strategy, engaging a maximum number of leaders through purposeful enlistment and organization of the groups, and moving to an outward focus has changed the culture of the Sunday school at Inola Baptist Church. The congregation has elected to pursue excellence instead of settling for mediocrity and allowing decline to overtake the congregation. Decline is the precursor of death, and though the church will never die, a congregation can vanish. It has already happened to many congregations in North America that once flourished.

Inola was a church that was hurting and insecure just a couple of short years ago. Like other congregations, they were good-hearted people who found the attendance dwindling in numbers. Over the past two years, church attendance has increased by over twenty percent and almost forty people came to faith in Jesus last year. The transformation of the Sunday school has been critical. The growth has come from the hand of God, but it was the Sunday school that was touched through the faithful leadership of a pastor and the engagement of committed members. The church has now embraced excellence in Sunday school as its standard of ministry. The Sunday school council states that by pursuing excellence and establishing a strategy, the church is encouraged as it sees God work through them, and realize they can see the results of their work.

The choice to do what it takes to thrive has been largely affected by the commitment to have a Sunday school ministry that really excels.

# CHAPTER 12

# Excels in Multicultural Community

## Leroy Gainey

MULTICULTURAL SUNDAY SCHOOL EVANGELISM IS as old as the United States of America itself. The United States of America was founded upon the principles of religious liberty. The subject of multicultural evangelism is not limited to the efforts of blacks and whites in evangelistic opportunities only. When people are exposed to Jesus and his model of evangelism, it is difficult not to see an intentional model of evangelism from God himself that reaches across racial, cultural, gender, and age boundary lines. The intercultural realignment so prevalent in North America today compels the follower of Jesus Christ to implement and model multicultural evangelistic efforts without reservation. Doing so through Sunday school is not the only way to reach people with the story of Jesus. However, the opportunity is presented to not only reach out but also to engage in dialogue with believers on what it really means to reach all nations as commanded in the Great Commission.

Let's take a brief journey back to see the roots of some of the challenges that we are faced with in accomplishing this great task. With the growth of African slavery as it swept the thirteen colonies, slaves and masters found themselves in a peculiar situation when it came to being the Christian church. Black slave congregants and white congregants worshiped in the same facilities, but usually in different areas. Ordinarily the back of the church or the balcony was reserved for slaves. Black slaves came to know Jesus Christ through their encounters alongside their slave masters, but they also grew in faith as well and reached out to other black slaves through secret worship services held in the brush arbors and in other places beyond the hearing distance of their masters. This is not to say that Christianity was not a part of the middle passage. We have evidence that Christian influence in Africa goes at least as far back as Philip and the Ethiopian encounter, but I believe that the story of Christ in Africa goes back even further in scriptures that speak to Christ's escape to Africa to avoid murder at the hands of King Herod.

In looking back to Christianity in America, in a sense, two kinds of evangelism were taking place simultaneously. The white Christian slave owners were sometimes evangelizing their black slaves and black slaves were evangelizing one another. These two kinds of evangelism took place until the end of the American Civil War when black denominations appeared and soon became more prominent in the United States as well as the attempts at eradicating illiteracy.

Most multicultural church growth was hindered by a system of racial division that existed in America from the end of the Civil War in 1865 until the passage of the Civil Rights Act in 1965. Few examples of truly multicultural congregations were to be found the two decades that followed. The truly multicultural church doesn't appear until the 1980s in the United States. Multicultural congregations are defined in this sense as those churches with a large percentage of congregants being made up of both black and white and other racial groups, having an ethnic senior pastor, and employing an intentional evangelistic ministry of reaching all peoples in their community. We are seeing more and more multicultural communities and the question is, how are existing churches going to reach these new people groups that are not across the world but in our own backyards?

Certainly, some churches are achieving diversity naturally, meaning they are not doing anything strategically to be multicultural. It is happening of its own volition. Still others have an intentional ministry of evangelism that reaches across racial divides. With the phenomenon of multicultural growth in the United States since 1965, there also comes the need for understanding how to reach this diversity of people with the gospel, as well as sustain this type of church growth.

The Scripture compels believers to heed the call of God on their lives to reach across racial and cultural lines with the gospel of Jesus Christ. A multicultural approach to Sunday school evangelism can address both aspects of intercultural missions and American diversity issues. Intercultural ministry focuses upon one culture attempting to penetrate another culture with the gospel. Multicultural Sunday school evangelism is the intentional effort to reach a multiplicity of racial groups living in one community. Discover who is in your community and determine to reach them whether or not they fit your own unique culture or your own comfort zone of ministry.

## REACHING DIFFERENT TYPES OF PEOPLE

The heart of the leaders seeking to minister in a multicultural setting should be to minister to all people without discrimination or partiality. However, it is true that different cultures attribute different values to similar issues such as time, styles of preaching, worship formats, and so forth. One is neither right while the other is wrong—nor is one superior to the other. People have varying tastes within cultures as well as between cultures. Understanding these values while resisting the temptation to place one's own preferences as exclusive or as spiritually superior is critical to effectively ministering cross-culturally. A mission's strategy requires a study of the culture that the missionary is reaching *out* to and reaching *in* to. Sunday school leaders must be willing to study and understand other cultures if they are to reach across cultural lines within their own communities.

You must begin by engaging individuals from other cultures seeking to develop friendships. Make observations and ask questions. You may find someone in your congregation that has an existing relationship with those that you seek to reach. Bear in mind, however, that their preferences, likes, and dislikes may differ from those of your congregation or Sunday school class. Are you willing to make some adjustments and some sacrifices if the result is that others can come into a faith relationship with Jesus because of your witness? You may find that some of the adjustments while minimal on your part may be major in lowering boundaries that might keep someone from connecting and hear the good news of Jesus.

Do you know who is in your community? Have you sought out demographic information about the area surrounding your church in recent years? This type of information is readily available and often at no cost or very low cost. Contact your local association, denominational leaders, or local government entities to discover what information is available. Look at your congregation and your group or Sunday school class. Does it look like the community? Or is it possible that over time your congregation has melded into a group with experience and background that is all the same while inadvertently excluding those who are different? Yet, for whom Christ also died on the cross and desires for your congregation to seek out.

Once you discover or acknowledge who is in your community and you begin to learn their unique values, customs, and preferences you can employ ministries taking those distinctives into consideration. Keep in mind that there are no methods that are fail-proof, and it is easy to miss the mark when ministering to a culture that you have not grown up with.

## PROMOTING YOUR CHURCH IN A MULTICULTURAL SETTING

It is important to let the multicultural community know that your church and your Bible study groups are open to all members of the community. They must also know that they are not only invited, but that they will be welcomed. Whatever means you use to attract that community, the promotion must be clear that you're no respecter of persons. For example, let us say you're having a block party, and you want people to come from a variety of racial backgrounds. It will then be necessary to have activities, music, food, etc., that will let your guests know that you're sensitive to the things that they enjoy. You cannot effectively reach across cultures by inviting people to come and join you in doing what you enjoy.

Using these kinds of broad methods immediately communicates to people that you value diversity, and by your intentional methodologies, you're willing to make relationships. Some of the easiest times to do multiracial evangelism is to have regular Christmas, Easter, and other holiday programs, but with the added touch of diversity as mentioned above. You can break out of this mold by how you promote your ministries and having something that specifically meets the needs of the persons you're trying to reach. The same can be said of your church website, as well as any other means you use to advertise who your church is and what it has to offer. If you aren't presently using some type of promotion, then you are really leaving it up to your community to define who you are.

## BARRIERS IN A MULTICULTURAL SETTING

Trying to reach too many people groups at one time will be difficult. Discover the largest people group in your community that are not engaged with your congregation and begin with them. Focus on the needs of one group at a time, or you won't meet the needs of any, and your efforts may be wasted. Learn the characteristics and values of one people group at a time while committing to make needed adjustments to reach out to them in sharing Christ and making disciples. Diversity can take hold as you penetrate that first group, and then you can expand to reach other groups that are part of your community. Help those who do connect likewise to learn to sacrifice for reaching other people groups. This strategy works, because as the congregation increases quantitatively, and all the people grow qualitatively, you'll be better able to reach different people as you have learned how important it is to sacrifice some of your culture to reach another culture.

First Baptist Church of Vacaville, California, has done this so many times that it is now the natural way of doing ministry. Change is difficult for any organization, but when you can see the results for the good of the kingdom of God, you become willing to give up all for the sake of Christ. I am convinced that this is what real love is—when you're willing to give up and share your lifestyle for the sake of another entering the family of God.

The Word of God teaches that our work is to make disciples (Matt. 28:18–20). Just telling people about Christ is not enough. We must welcome them into the family of God and help them to grow in their relationship with Jesus. This will be a challenge because we will not only have to adapt our methods in reaching people, but we will also have to change how we educate people in order to assimilate the people God sends us. Here are some examples:

**Teaching and Preaching:** When teaching and preaching in a diverse setting, it is important to practice using instructional designs that clearly communicate that you, as a facilitator, respect the cultural backgrounds of the audience. You should utilize pictures, stories, and as many other depictions that you can that represent the audience's background more so than your own. There is a tendency in teaching to use illustrations from your own background and not take into consideration that your audience may be unfamiliar or uninterested in just hearing about your own personal experiences. In addition, whatever illustrations you use should be positive in nature. Negative and stereotypical images will communicate that you are not in touch with the changing world around you and may even reinforce a negative behavior in your listeners. The same can be said when you attempt to be neutral in your presentation by not using any cultural depictions in your teaching or preaching instructional design. Your audience may feel as if you are not in touch with their reality and come to feel as if you don't value their cultural perspective.

**Leadership Development:** Leadership development should be presented in such a manner that all those in your membership feel as if they have an opportunity to ascend to the heights of ministry that God has for them. This can be accomplished best by having opportunities where all of the people get a chance to stretch their skills and talents. If the practice and playing field is even, and you don't play favorites, then everyone will understand that God shows no partiality based on culture. This means providing an opportunity for your diverse constituency, as well as gender differences and generational differences, to learn how to do ministry without any constraints. Your assessments ought to be fair and without discrimination based on race or culture. The challenges to develop ought to be extended to all members.

And the support that you provide ought to be rich in elements that communicate that all of God's children are called to be the best that they can be for God. This clearly communicates that God is no respecter of persons and neither are the members of the congregation.

**Respect for Other Cultures:** Efforts to reach all kinds of people are noble efforts. These efforts are in keeping with Scripture to do evangelism as Jesus did and honor the depiction of what heaven is going to look like. Unlike homogenous churches, the multicultural type of church needs much assistance in the areas of balance, conflict management, leadership development, and opportunities for personal growth.

The reference at this point relates more to health than strategy. Multicultural churches can experience growth while at the same time being unhealthy. Examples of this would be churches that have individuals who deny their racial identity all together, as well as their respective histories. Assimilation to the point where one group begins to start acting like another group, dressing like another group, and/or talking like another group in order to remain together may not be healthy. This can inadvertently lead to a lack of appreciation for diversity. People possess various strengths and weaknesses related to experience, education, intellect, passions, and spiritual giftedness. God did not design everyone the same and does not intend that everyone be alike. Believers are to be one in spirit, unified in faith, and holding to a common confession in Jesus Christ as Savior and Lord. Beyond that, there is strength in diversity of all of the aforementioned as well as with race and culture. What makes a genuine multicultural congregation vibrant is their respect for diversity and the desire of the congregation to discover new ways to help all groups find their worth in Christ. Some of the avenues that engender health include the following:

**Balance and Conflict Management:** Seek balance in your group's evangelistic efforts so that different people can be reached across the spectrum of possibilities. This can be achieved by as little effort as sending out those doing intentional ministry in pairs or triads of multicultural/racial makeup. Be prepared for conflict because the probability of conflict is greater when differences are more readily apparent. Teaching and learning the art of compromise and turn-taking is a great asset in these instances.

## FIRST BAPTIST CHURCH OF VACAVILLE, CALIFORNIA

Obviously, it is easier to reach people when you adhere to the homogenous principle of people liking to be with people who are like them. The most obvious consideration is that people who are different racially today may, in fact, be more closely aligned with people who are different than they are racially, but more similar culturally. The racial divide may be just as wide as it has ever been, but the cultural divide is shrinking. From the perspective of music, clothing, language, food, entertainment, and education, the differences are minimizing. The fact remains that people may still want to be with people of their own heritage, and that is their preference. This means that there will, in all probability, always be a place for homogenous church development. The Bible does not forbid this type of evangelism, and it is admittedly easier to reach out to those to whom you are most familiar. The aim is not to destroy what you have if it is effective in reaching people, but to adapt to reach as many as God will enable you to reach. You may even have to be honest in acknowledging that your group or church is not effective in reaching any as it is. God knows hearts as well as our abilities, and you should take full advantage of your strengths. The most important thing is to boldly reach people for Jesus Christ. God has given Christendom in the United States an unprecedented opportunity to use the multicultural racial strategy in sharing the gospel that did not exist prior to the 1970s.

First Baptist Church of Vacaville, California is an excellent example of a church that has been able to overcome cultural barriers to reach out to many cultures and to have a Sunday school that excels in doing so. Here are some examples of how they made it happen:

1. By elevating people of different cultures in to key roles of leadership in the congregation

2. By espousing a theology that emphasizes the admonition of the Great Commission to make disciples "of all nations" beginning in their own community

3. By prioritizing Sunday school as an environment intentionally designed to aid in cultural interaction and growth through leveraging small group dynamics and continually creating new groups

4. By seeking styles of music that do not favor a particular ethnic group while blending music on occasion that affirms value of all represented groups

5. By implementing technologies that afford the option of hearing messages in the heart language of the hearer

6. By being attentive to conflicts as they emerge and focusing on biblical means of resolution

7. By implementing a comprehensive evangelism strategy that is needs-based, focused on the unique values of each culture being touched

8. By displaying love and acceptance of all people desiring to meet needs, sharing Jesus, and making disciples of all

## CONCLUSIONS

Doing multicultural Sunday School-Evangelism can be the most challenging and exciting type of ministry today. It fits the model of what God says heaven will ultimately look like. It looks like the reconciliation depiction that Christ so vigorously lived and died for. It is the gospel of Jesus Christ incarnate today. The momentary challenges of cultural conflict do not outweigh the significant consequences of people of diversity working together for the kingdom's sake. Nothing communicates clearer the love of Christ than people loving one another. There will always be homogeneous congregations, but heterogeneous congregations raise the bar concerning what the Lord is expecting of the church.

You can't develop this kind of church without God's help. Perhaps that is why the Lord has established the cultural divide—not to keep us apart, but to understand that we can't achieve oneness with one another or with him without his guiding hand. While the Bible commands the church to go into all of the world, there are many communities in North America where the world is coming to them. It is happening all around us naturally. The opportunity for ministry is one where there is no failure. The only failure is not trying. The church of the future in North America in a multicultural community will become more the norm than a phenomenon. Perhaps your Sunday school is being called by God to excel in reaching people in a multicultural community. It is being done in Vacaville, California, and it can happen in your community too if you will follow God's lead.

# CHAPTER 13

# Excels in Transitioning to Small Groups

## *Elmer Towns*

DAVE EARLEY, A 1985 LIBERTY University graduate, planted a church in the greater Columbus, Ohio area—New Life Community Baptist Church, Gahanna, Ohio. Earley was one of the first church planters from Liberty to plant a church utilizing a team of staff from the outset. There were five on the team including Rod Dempsey, a Liberty Baptist Theological Seminary graduate, who served as the Sunday school director.

More than twenty-five years have passed since those five young men with little more than big dreams and the willingness to step out on faith went to greater Columbus, Ohio, to plant New Life Community Baptist Church. Two weeks following graduation, Earley and his team loaded their few belongings and young brides into two U-Haul rental trucks and pulled out of Lynchburg in route to the suburbs of Columbus. Starting with eleven people, New Life Community Baptist Church has become one of the largest and fastest growing churches in the Columbus area.

Initially, only senior pastor Dave Earley was full time, living on six months of support raised from pastor friends and Liberty

Baptist Fellowship of Church Planting. The other men—Rod Dempsey, Steve Benninger, Chris Brown, and Brian Robertson—worked various secular jobs as the church grew. In less than five years, all five men were on staff full time, giving oversight to a variety of ministries. All five Liberty grads were still with the church ten years later. Pastor Earley observes, "We tried to practice biblical relationships. Being committed to one another has made it possible for us to grow as individuals and as a team."

Dave Earley's vision of making disciples in a member-centered ministry is what originally drew the team together. Nearly eighty percent of New Life's members serve in ministry each week. The pastors view their own roles to be primarily that of coaches and equippers, rather than ministers. "We give leadership; the people do ministry." Most of those who attend New Life are baby boomers; many from unchurched backgrounds. New Life has baptized an average of fifty people every year.

In order to make disciples, New Life has four primary meeting times each week: Celebrations, Congregations, Cells, and New Community. There are three celebration services each Sunday, traditionally called the worship service. The first is traditional in style while the other two are contemporary and seeker-sensitive in nature, incorporating a worship band and drama team.

## OVERCOMING SPACE CHALLENGES

In 1995, the church built (then ten years old) their second worship center designed to accommodate one thousand people. "Even though they built twice," Rod Dempsey noted, "we ran out of Sunday school space." The church added an additional worship service for growth, but the lack of Sunday school rooms limited the church's growth. Additional facilities were built including a Family Life Center, but overcrowded parking, full Sunday school classrooms, and congested hallways continued to create challenges.

The rapid expansion of facilities also created other challenges. Rod Dempsey noted, "We had just built a $2 million building, but we were $2 million in debt, and couldn't borrow any more money for additional adult education space." How do you grow a Sunday school ministry when you do not have the facilities to do so?

The staff started talking about how small groups could serve as an answer for space challenges. "We went back to examine what we had done in *our college and seminary days* at Liberty University when Dave was the campus pastor and oversaw hundreds of small groups." Dempsey stated, "It was really back to the future. ... We envisioned small groups meeting in homes instead of college students meeting in dorm rooms."

"Dave gave me permission to investigate further, so I traveled.... I went to Willow Creek in South Barrington, Illinois, to see what they did there. I went to Saddleback in California to see what they did. I read Yonggi Cho's book on *Successful Home Cell Groups* to examine how he built the largest church in the world through small groups. I went to hear Joel Comiskey who had written many books on the cell group movement. Then I went to a conference in Tucson, Arizona, and spoke with him personally. The other person I spoke with was Larry Stockstill [at] Bethany World Prayer Center, Baton Rouge, Louisiana." In addition, Dempsey started searching the scriptures to study how small groups got started in the early church. He asked himself the basic question, "What does the Bible say about making disciples?" He came to the conclusion, "Jesus made disciples through small groups."

Dempsey continued by studying the phrases in scripture associated with "one another"—i.e., love one another, exhort one another, counsel one another, and pray for one another. He noted, "We could accomplish the relationships found in 'one another' in small groups, more than in traditional Sunday school. Sunday school has a very strong educational component as far as teaching the Word of God, but the fellowship component was not as strong as was found in groups that met in homes. Sunday school was driven by content, while small groups in the home are driven by relationships. The 'one anothers' lend themselves very well to being accomplished in a smaller, more intimate setting … in someone's home. The idea of discipleship had more to do with the idea of following Jesus, not just learning more and more information or content. Small groups are not so much content driven but application driven."

Dempsey said, "I saw very clearly in the book of Acts that the early church practiced house church, or home church, or small groups that met in homes. The more I studied church history, the more I understood. They met in homes for the most part for the first three hundred years." So he concluded, "In our suburb of Columbus, Ohio, we believed we could begin to develop some small groups that met in homes."

Please note at this point that the church did not begin to dismantle the Sunday school (the children and youth Sunday schools were kept and strengthened as the small groups began to grow) nor did they totally transition away from adult Sunday school. They began calling the Sunday morning groups ABCs—Adult Bible Congregations—and kept adult groups going during the Sunday school hour.

However, Dempsey began looking at developing several small groups meeting in homes in addition to their Sunday school. "That first year we had about ten adult Sunday school classes meeting on our campus on Sunday morning and seven small groups meeting in homes. The next year increased to about twenty-five small groups. Then we started noticing that our Sunday school classes were paring down; we went from ten classes down to seven or eight. The next year we had about fifty small groups, and then by the third year in, we had about seventy-five adult groups but only one or two adult Sunday school classes meeting on Sunday morning."

Within four years of the transition, the church had more than one hundred small groups. The change to small groups took about five years and was complete when Dempsey resigned to take a teaching position at his alma mater. The Sunday morning focused educational model evolved into a small group model with 125 groups and seventeen coaches that gave leadership and oversight.

## SERMON-BASED CURRICULUM

The church learned from Joel Comiskey and Paul Yonggi Cho that small groups work well when connected to the senior pastor's Sunday morning message. Therefore, the church developed sermon-based groups. When a member came on Sunday morning, he or she heard the message and then went to a group on Monday night to discuss and apply the Word. Dempsey noted, "We call it kind of a one-two punch: They hear it on Sunday morning, and hear more during the week, but the focus during the week was how to apply it. The groups discuss their ideas with one another and learn from one another. Hence, it is a relational group.

"Dave Earley is an excellent pulpit Bible teacher, so we had great small group discussions. But in some churches, the preaching/teaching is topical or light on content, not much depth. When the church had a guest speaker that was motivational, or didn't have content, our team of leaders had to supplement the message and get the additional lesson outlines to the groups."

If churches are going to make this transition to small groups, then Dempsey recommends connecting the Sunday morning sermon to the weekday Bible study groups. There are several advantages to sermon-based groups:

1. It keeps the senior pastor in the lead teaching position.

2. It prevents groups from getting off base doctrinally.

3. It aids in recruiting leaders, as they need not possess strong teaching skills to lead a discussion of the pastor's message.

4. It keeps the entire church on one thought, one central idea for the week.

5. It aids in application as group members discuss how they can apply the message.

## LEADER ENLISTMENT

"Leaders for small groups come from small groups." Dempsey explains. "We like to think of it as a farm-team system. You don't normally begin playing baseball in New York for the Yankees; you spend several seasons down in the farm teams. We would not let a small group start without an apprentice. There's a difference between an assistant and an apprentice. An assistant helps the leader, and an apprentice is being trained to take over the group at some point. Usually, we recommend three leadership positions: small group leader, small group apprentice, and small group host. Those are three separate persons. We also added another layer of leadership, which is a coaching layer, but we didn't require that at the beginning."

## CHANGES AT LIBERTY

Thomas Road Baptist Church in Lynchburg, Virginia is well known for its Christian university and the ministry of the late Dr. Jerry Falwell. The outsider might think of the church as very traditional, but you may be surprised to discover the changes that they have experienced in their education ministry in recent years. Once Dr. Dempsey returned to Liberty to serve on the university staff, he was also tapped to serve as the discipleship director for the church.

The incorporation of a small group approach did not happen immediately, given the strong tradition of the Sunday school ministry at the church. The construction of a new educational facility opened the door to introduce some new innovations initially. The first phase of change was built on the idea of "community outreach groups." These were service groups, engaging large numbers of congregation members in service and servant community evangelism opportunities. The groups were developed into teams and launched out of homes of members as well as from the church campus.

The groups varied in their focus ranging from ministries like Alzheimer support groups, a Ruth Brooks Free Medical Clinic, free legal advice, scrapbooking, golf groups, and computer training. A variety of these ministry groups met on campus on Wednesday nights utilizing the talents, gifts, hobbies, interests, and skill sets of the members. In addition, group leaders with expertise or specialization from the community were invited to provide leadership in some of the ministry groups.

Traditional prayer meeting services continued to meet on Wednesday evenings with almost as many people participating in the various ministry and interest groups. The prayer meeting was connected and served as a base of prayer support for the various groups. The groups, in this phase, were not intended to substitute for involvement in Sunday school but to supplement avenues of service and community outreach opportunities in which members could participate. Falwell referred to involvement in these groups as "spiritual glue" that got many members involved in using the gifts and talents to minister and to do the work of evangelism.

## MOVING FROM COMMUNITY GROUPS TO SMALL GROUPS

A new generation of leadership emerged when Jonathan Falwell was called to serve in the same pulpit as his late father in 2007. Like his father, he was convinced that the church needed to involve as many people as possible in serving and advancing the Kingdom. The support of the ministry groups continued, but a renewed emphasis on Sunday morning groups was initiated. Facilities were available to grow the Sunday school ministry at this point, and the primary focus returned to bolstering Sunday mornings. New Sunday school units were created, and the growth came with the renewed priority.

Within three years, the church found that they were totally out of any more space to expand the Sunday school. The congregation was blessed with a great season of growth and evangelistic results during this season. The number of people coming to know Jesus as Savior and the number of people joining the church could not be absorbed into the existing structure. The church staff knew that the creation of new groups would be critical to minister to those being reached and to continue to reach others.

The decision to utilize weekday small groups to supplement Sunday school was made in order to address the space limitations. A staff was assigned responsibility, consultation was made with successful, small group leaders, and a campaign was launched to promote the effort. Liberty Baptist Church is known for large adult Sunday school classes. The small groups multiplied the number of units more than tenfold. Liberty Baptist offers a combination of Sunday school classes that meet on Sunday morning and small groups that meet throughout the week.

Making a transition to small groups for the church with an established Sunday school requires tough decisions. Liberty Baptist learned that the strategy of "small groups" does not encompass a single approach. A congregation making a change must determine whether the transition will go to cell groups or serendipity-style groups or campaign-style groups. However, the key question is whether you're going to be (1) a church *with* groups, (2) a church that is *of* groups, or (3) a church that *is* groups. A church *with* groups is the traditional church that primarily has Sunday morning groups that meet on the church's property. When a church desires to transition to *of* groups, it begins to offer groups that meet at a variety of times and in a variety of places. The focus is still on Sunday morning, and the church is usually attracting or "come and see" in nature, but there is a concerted effort to get everyone in a group. A church that desires to transition to become a church that *is* groups is looking to reboot the entire operating system of the church. The focus becomes the development of disciples in groups and homes. This is very similar to a house church movement.

## STEPS TO SMALL GROUPS

In order to make the transition, Rod Dempsey created an outline for his doctoral thesis, *Transitioning a Traditional Educational Model to a Small Groups System*[1] and developed an acrostic based on: S. M. A. L. L. G. R. O. U. P. S.

### 1. Seek God's Vision

The first step is critical. The best place to go to receive God's vision is to go to God. One of the primary ways a person goes to God is to go to his Word. By studying the passages outlined in this project that relate to accomplishing the Great Commission, the Great Commandment, and the New Commandment, church leaders can reach their own conclusions about what type of disciple making system they plan to produce, "spiritually mature zealots who are able to reproduce."[2]

The other place to go to receive God's vision for your ministry is to wait silently before the Lord in prayer. Jesus was very clear about the nature of prayer when he said the following, "But you, when you pray, go into your room, and when you have shut

---

1.   Rod Dempsey, *Transitioning a Traditional Educational Model to a Small Groups System* (D.Min., Liberty Baptist Theological Seminary, 2004).
2.   George Barna, *Growing True Disciples* (Ventura, CA: Regal Books, 2003), 32.

your door, pray to your Father who is in the secret place; and your Father who sees in secret will reward you openly" (Matt. 6:6).

## 2. Make Sure the Pastor is in the Lead Position

Without the senior pastor's full support and involvement, any significant ministry is doomed to mediocrity. It really is foolish to undertake a significant ministry shift or change without the senior pastor being fully on board. It is incumbent upon the senior pastor to be in the lead position. Ultimately, he is given the responsibility to "[s]hepherd the flock of God which is among you" (1 Peter 5:2). The greater responsibility for discipling and shepherding the flock will be on their shoulders when pastors stand before God and give an account for the flock that the Chief Shepherd has entrusted to their care (See Hebrews 13:17).

In addition, the person doing the feeding, usually the senior pastor, is also the person with the greatest amount of influence on the individual member of the church. When the senior pastor speaks, people listen. John Maxwell calls this, "The Law of E. F. Hutton."[3] The main reason for this is simple. This is the person who on a weekly basis breaks the bread of life to the members, and they regularly experience God speaking to them through their pastor's ministry. The pastor is God's spokesperson for the hour. As a result, when the pastor speaks about small groups or really about any subject, the members will more often than not listen to the instructions and directions from God's under shepherd. It is also particularly powerful when the senior pastor can mention a small group story or a small group victory to illustrate and punch a point in the sermon. The small group pastor can have a definite role and impact in the effective organization and running of the ministry, but the senior pastor must be the primary force and cheerleader for the ministry.

---

3.   John Maxwell, *The 21 Irrefutable Laws of Leadership* (Nashville, TN: Thomas Nelson, 2007), 43.

### 3. Adopt a Model That Fits Who and Where You Are

Gene Getz has said that "Christian theology must be done in the context of the local church."[4] Ultimately the implications, ramifications, and applications of the Scripture must be grasped by a group of believers in a local church. For local church leaders, it means that it is important to take into consideration before adopting any approach or methodology what is the church's ministry, history, location, and context. For instance, if as a pastor, say in Birmingham, Alabama (or some other city in the South where Sunday school has been the one and only method of disciple making), one should think twice about adopting a new, fangled approach to ministry. If the pastor is convinced that a transition is needed, then that pastor will also understand that 'patience' is needed and that taking the long view is in order. The apostle Paul put it this way:

> and to the Jews I became as a Jew, that I might win Jews; to those who are under the law, as under the law, that I might win those who are under the law; to those who are without law, as without law (not being without law toward God, but under law toward Christ), that I might win those who are without law; to the weak I became as weak, that I might win the weak. I have become all things to all men, that I might by all means save some (1 Cor. 9:20–22).

If a ministry transitions to a small group strategy, then that ministry must adopt a model that fits the church's context.

### 4. Leader Recruitment and Training

Everything rises and falls on leadership. This is particularly true in regard to transitioning to a small group system. The

---

4.   Presentation of Gene Getz, "Growing True Disciples" Conference, San Diego CA, February 2003, Rod Dempsey's personal notes, Forest, VA.

pastors or the church leaders in the local church must do everything in their power to seek out and find those people who have leadership capability, and then they must train them to be as effective as they can be.

It starts with a "holy discomfort" of having people sit week after week in your church and not grow and develop into all that they can be. A small group system forces pastors to view many people as potential leaders. Romans 12 and 1 Corinthians 12 are good passages to study and understand that God desires all the gifts in the body to be functioning. This means that church leaders must develop systems both at the macro level and micro level that will encourage and enable many people to get involved in the Great Commission. This does not mean that only members with the gift of teaching can be involved in leading small groups. People with the spiritual gift of "helps" make excellent small group leaders. Likewise, people with the gift of mercy make excellent small group leaders. In fact, with the exception of the prophet, just about every spiritual gift enables a person to lead a small group effectively. The training should not be so difficult or long that the average church member would be intimidated. Jesus's method of leadership training works well here: Teach them a little bit, then send them out. When they come back, teach them some more.

### 5. Launch the New Ministry

The word *launch* means "to slide" a new vessel into the water/to set in operation or on some course; start something new; to plunge into.[5] Sliding your new vessel (small groups) into the water takes quite a bit of faith. Are there holes in the vessel? Is it sea worthy? What if it does not float? Maybe these are some of the emotions one may experience as the new,

---

5. *Webster's New World Dictionary and Thesaurus* (New York: Simon and Schuster, 1996), s.v. "launch."

small group ministry transition is launched. Inevitably, the new vessel must be pushed out into the water and watched. It has to begin sometime. It could begin with a fall kickoff event for the first five or six groups. It could be a sermon series where the biblical value of being in groups is preached, and then the new ministry is begun. It could be possible to bring in a nationally known speaker or small group leader to launch the new groups. Perhaps, one could begin with an elder or deacon's meeting where the concept is presented with a question and answer period. Eventually though, after the prayer, study, and planning, the new ministry has to be launched out into the deep.

There will be leaks along the way, but if prepared properly, and if corrections are made as the ministry progresses, in no time at all the ministry will be sailing to new and exciting vistas. Once new, positive results emerge, the effort will have been worth it all.

### 6. Grow the Quantity and Quality of the Groups

A person may ask which one is more important, quantity or quality? They are both equally important. Initially, during the launch phase, it is very important to grow the quantity of groups so that the new ministry can develop some natural momentum. Leaders should do whatever it takes to get new people involved in small groups.

Later on, it is important to develop substantial quality, because people will only attend a poorly led group for so long. This is why good small group leaders are so important. If a leader stops doing the little things well, then the group is in trouble, because "people don't care how much you know until they know how much you care."

### 7. Reward the Right Behavior

Mark Twain once said, "I can for two months on a good

compliment."[6] This is true for most people. Yet, the natural tendency is to focus on the wrong things observed in people or in their small group. One way to compliment right behavior is during a quarterly small group rally. Take time to review progress and ask coaches about which leader was doing a good job, and then highlight the person or the group during the rally time. Upon talking glowingly about the person or groups, one can literally see appreciation flowing into the person or group. As others take note of the positive behavior, they are encouraged and emboldened to do likewise. Showing appreciation in a small group transition strategy is invaluable.

## 8. Overcommunicate

People like to feel like they are a part of something exciting. Poor communication causes people to grow suspicious of leaders and the new ministry. Here are a few communication ideas.

- Preach a series on small groups.

- Create a small group newsletter for members and leaders.

- Send emails every week to small group leaders.

- Periodically, feed the senior pastor great stories about small groups so that he can do a "message mention."

- Teach a lesson in the new members' class on the importance of getting connected to a small group.

- Send basic phone reminders to your leaders.

---

6. http://quotationsbook.com/quote/7666/#sthash.YyewOBBH.dpbs (accessed April 2013).

- Have a running monthly column in the main newsletter for the church.

Most small group ministries suffer from undercommunication. Rick Warren has quipped, "People are down on what they are not up on."[7] The problem with undercommunication is that it kills enthusiasm and momentum. Leaders of a small group system must do whatever is necessary to get the word out about what is happening.

### 9. Utilize and Develop Coaches

The coaching system is the key to effective functioning of a small group strategy. Without a coaching system, small groups will decline and could even cause problems. Your coaches are the key to a successful long-term small group ministry. Championship teams have great coaches. Championship teams are usually led by effective coaches who know how to get the most out of their players. In most situations, successful coaches are ex-players. In a small group system, the coaches need to at least have led a group successfully, and hopefully they have even multiplied their group several times. It is prudent not to select and use coaches who have not successfully led small groups.

Furthermore, small groups by their very nature are de-centralized and usually meet off campus. This opens the door for many issues. The coaches had better be getting around to see what is happening in the groups. Coaches make sure that groups and group leaders are on track with the overall vision and mission of the church. They also protect the church from doctrinal error and divisive issues if they are functioning. Coaches are essential to develop powerful long-term groups.

---

7. Rick Warren, Saddleback Conference, 2001; Rod Dempsey's personal notes.

### 10. Pray

Prayer must be the central component in a small group strategy. It must be the central strategy in any church work because even though it is almost a cliché, "Nothing of eternal significance is ever accomplished apart from prayer."[8] There are two levels where prayer must be pervasive.

The small group pastor and leadership team should be praying for workers/laborers to be sent into the ministry. Jesus said, "Therefore pray the Lord of the harvest to send out laborers into His harvest" (Matt. 9:38). If a church is not specifically praying for new leaders, then that church will not discover them. God wants a leader and a ministry to pray according to his will (1 John 5:14–15), and he wants believers to pray specifically. The small group pastor must be praying for new leaders. The small group leader should be praying at least an hour a day for their flock and their needs. Studies have been done that reveal the groups that successfully multiply, are the groups in which the leader is praying an hour a day.[9] Small group leaders need to set the example for the members in their group. They need to be praying daily for the members of their group.

The small group pastor and leader can always tell when a small group leader is praying. That leader and that group is going to be reporting answers to prayer, the group is going to be growing, potential leaders are being mentored, and the group is exciting. God is answering prayer.

### 11. See God and Expand Your Vision

Making the transition from a Sunday school system to a small group ministry is not easy, but when you see more disciples growing and more leaders developing, you realize that

---

8. Quote of Dr. Jerry Falwell, http://trbc.org/insidetrbc/prayer-ministry (last accessed 4/23/13).
9. Jay Firebaugh and Ralph Neighbour, Jr., Cell-Group Conference, Houston, Texas, 2002.

God is at work, and greater things can be accomplished. In the Great Commission, Jesus, has given us this promise, "I am with you always, even to the end of the age" (Matt. 28:20). If you are serious about developing God's children, then you will seriously experience his favor in your life, in your church, and in your community.

# CHAPTER 14

# Excels at Combining Traditional Sunday School and Innovative Home Groups

## Tim S. Smith

THE FLAMING DEBATE BETWEEN THOSE singularly supportive of traditional Sunday school and those who propose innovative small groups (home groups) continues to be fanned into a full-blown inferno. There are those on both sides that possess an either/or mentality. Some churches have taken a different approach by asking, "Why not both?"

Consider first the merits of Sunday morning Bible study groups. The traditional Sunday school has a proven track record of effectiveness. It is an effective tool for assimilation of new members as well as new comers but only if the group is aggressive with consistent expressions of love and concern for the members. Traditional Sunday school works best for families with children from birth to middle school. The demands of life usually make it very challenging for those families with children to be involved beyond Sunday morning by adding another night during the week for a small group experience. Traditional Sunday school allows for children and teens to be involved with both corporate worship and a small group. In some instances, with the design of a home group strategy, the children and students are left out, or their small group experience is conducted while the adults are in corporate worship on Sundays. If both corporate worship and the small group experience are vital for adults, then it is even more essential for children and teens.

Innovative small groups or home groups that gather at times other than Sunday morning have a very valuable contribution to make with today's church. This approach is very appealing to those that have not grown up in church because meeting in a neighbor's or friend's home can be less threatening. The home environment also promotes a more intimate experience that results in the development of trusting friendships. Home groups also are advantageous in that they are less formal and not as constrained by time, resulting in more time for personal interaction within the group.

## LAKEWOOD CHURCH

Both approaches can be the source of frustration, and both have unique limitations. Each can serve as sources of frustration for church leaders as well. The success of either hinges on a common challenge. Whether your groups meet on Sunday morning on campus or in homes during the week, it is critical that leaders guide them to be missional in their purpose. An example of a church that has excelled with both traditional Sunday school and innovative home groups is Lakewood Baptist Church in Gainesville, Georgia.

The primary staff member responsible for the leadership of both is Scott Smith. The senior pastor is Tom Smiley, and he has been the pastor since 1990. Scott has been on the church staff since 2000. The church was founded in 1956, and had previously peaked at an attendance of around three hundred prior to Smiley's call as pastor. Attendance has increased an average of sixteen percent each year since he began, meaning the total attendance has more than doubled twice during that time.

## LAKEWOOD'S GROUP STRATEGY

Lakewood has both a traditional Sunday school and innovative home groups. The Sunday school ministry serves as the initial entry point into the church/community life. The corporate worship experience tends to be the first point of entry for guests desiring to become members of the church, but the Sunday school class is the beginning of their assimilation into the life of the church. The function of the traditional Sunday school is to aid people in feeling a sense of belonging, becoming connected to the church, and being part of a group which is genuinely expressing consistent, weekly care. The teaching of the Bible has a very high priority in the Sunday school with an emphasis on application.

The home groups are much smaller in size compared to the Sunday school classes. The typical Sunday school class has about seventeen in weekly attendance while the home group averages about eight each week. The home groups are much less formal than the Sunday school classes and are not limited in their time together each week. The content of the group study is ordinarily a video enhanced approach with much more discussion, and interaction is experienced more compared to the Sunday school classes.

Beginning an innovative small/home group ministry is not for the faint of heart, or for those unwilling to invest in the effort. Scott Smith said, "Working with home groups is three times the work load of leading Sunday school." The intimate environment of the home groups allows for transparency. When people begin to let down their guard, ministry can really begin, and community can be established. However, the leadership of the groups can be draining emotionally, physically, and spiritually as the transparency opens doors to a deeper involvement in the problems and challenges faced by group members. That dynamic can become a reality for staff who have responsibility for the groups as well as the home leaders. The acknowledgement of this dynamic is not to suggest that openness should not be encouraged, but a reminder that all ministry comes with challenges that will have to be addressed to maintain the spiritual health and morale of those given responsibility for leadership.

"Home groups usually become closed after four to six weekly gatherings," according to Scott Smith. Although the groups are more intimate, they tend to close, meaning that they are not as inclined to outreach or add new members once established. A traditional Sunday school class also has a tendency to close, but the window is much larger, taking from eighteen to twenty-four months to do so due to the fact that the group is more fluid with members and guests entering and exiting more regularly.

## CHALLENGES

The greatest challenge faced by Lakewood is the same that is faced by most church leaders—getting people into smaller groups beyond the large group worship experience. Many people today desire nothing more for their spiritual life than to attend a large group gathering like a dynamic worship experience. How do you convince members that they need to connect to a small group in order to experience real community? Many members are unaware that they are victims of a consumer mentality unique to contemporary culture that is based on what the church has to offer the individual rather than what the member can offer to the church. Therefore, home group leaders must go the extra mile of maintaining ministry contact with group members beyond the weekly gatherings if the groups are to succeed. Additional prayer needs can be discovered and responded to as a result of these extended efforts. Lakewood emphasizes this as well as attending to content. The consumer mentality will not abide lifeless teaching or boring experiences. Therefore, Lakewood guides group leaders to provide quality experiences that integrate openness, ministry to members, and relevant Bible teaching appropriate for those in attendance.

Lakewood also puts energy into developing new leaders and creating new groups as critical components of continued growth. Like all churches, the need for additional leaders is never-ending. The staff seeks to discover and train new leaders for new groups continually to create new groups and to replace existing home group leaders that need a break, as well as those that move out of the community. While the intimacy of the groups is desirable, the consequence is that some leaders get emotionally burned out. Lakewood seeks to be intentional in addressing this. One resource that is standard in their leadership development is a resource titled *Group Life Essentials: A Look at the Traits of Authentic Community*, which is designed to give leaders the tools they need to guide groups effectively and to endure by learning to give of themselves in a way that honors Christ.

## WHY LAKEWOOD EXCELS

Leadership is a critical component of success in any organization. God also uses leaders to shepherd his flock in local churches. Scott Smith is regarded as an excellent minister of education who has applied his gifts and skills to make both Sunday school and small groups excel in a single congregation. The pastor's leadership is even more critical in that he is the key voice for communicating vision and purpose. Tom Smiley is a long tenured pastor who has championed the importance of life in groups, be it Sunday morning or during the week, as well as the worship and preaching experience. He has not only provided the leadership but also developed others, including a staff who is committed to the vision of both Sunday morning and weekday groups.

Another factor that has led Lakewood to excel is a high priority on relationships. People are the focus. The leaders give more than lip service to relationships, which is not an uncommon point of emphasis in many churches. People are the priority at Lakewood, and they know that they matter. This priority is demonstrated through both the traditional Sunday school classes and the home groups. The Bible teaching is excellent, and the consistent, weekly expressions of care results in people being excited about their group. Scott Smith shares, "It's rare for people to miss a home group meeting." One member said, "If I miss, I'm afraid I'm going to miss something." They emphasize that discipleship (the process of spiritual growth) occurs through relationships and daily life, not in a classroom studying a prepackaged Christian resource.

Another factor that allows Lakewood to excel in their community is what Smith describes as "high accountability and low control." The staff has expectations of both group leaders and the groups. The expectations are communicated in the leadership training process developed by Smith. All leaders meet for eight sessions from September through May for two hours at each gathering. The expectations and desired performance levels of both leaders and groups are presented in these monthly sessions. The topics addressed include: Share (evangelism), Read (Bible study), Memorize, Pray, Eat (fellowship), Serve, Give, Care (ministry), and Multiply. Each group and group leader knows what is expected, but the aim is not to micromanage. The actions through which the leaders are tasked to accomplish these expectations are not specifically dictated. The groups and group leaders are provided suggestions but are encouraged to use their giftedness and the ideas of their group to determine their specific action plans to accomplish the mission. The monthly leadership gatherings also serve as a source of encouragement to the group leaders, providing motivation to carry out their objectives. The leaders know that the church and staff cares for them and is providing the tools needed to accomplish their task.

These regular gatherings are undergirded by a major "annual gathering" which also plays an important role in allowing Lakewood to excel. The focus of this meeting is multiplication and reproduction of leaders. Every group and every leader is expected to reproduce themselves in other groups and leaders. This action is demonstrated to them through the life and ministry of the minister of education, Scott Smith. He personally teaches an adult Sunday school class and leads a small group. The small group leaders of the weekday groups can all be traced back to the groups that he has led and the training that he has provided. Leaders develop other leaders, and the annual training, the on-going training, and the leadership of the staff brings new leaders forth to sustain the growth and enable the groups to excel.

## CONCLUSION

Sunday school and small groups bring unique challenges to the table, and providing both at one church is quite a stretch to the staff and leadership. But, it can be done. In an interview with Scott Smith, he summarized what he perceived to be the keys to excelling. It begins with an emphasis on "life change." Lakewood's approach to ministry includes a method to track the spiritual development of members. They have identified specific characteristics and actions desired in mature followers of Christ. Their curriculum is designed to lead a person through the development process, and they employ an assessment tool that aids in identifying areas of weakness in a member's spiritual development. Implementing a system such as this is high maintenance but high return, much like leading Sunday school and small groups.

Secondly, there is an emphasis on leader and group multiplication. Every adult group, both traditional Sunday school and innovative small groups, are expected to reproduce in eighteen to twenty-four months. In order to achieve this, every leader is expected to enlist an apprentice to receive "on the job" training.

Thirdly, there exists an emphasis on missional living. The people of the church must be living and telling the gospel message in their daily lives. This is an expectation for the members, and it is communicated and modeled by the leaders of the church. The programming of the church also reflects this by not requiring the members to constantly be on the church campus. They are encouraged to be on the mission field in the community instead of being on the church campus.

Smith makes the following recommendations to leaders who are contemplating creation of small groups as a component of their discipleship strategy, based on his experience at Lakewood:

+ **Think relationally.** The priority has got to be people.

+ **Don't think numerically.** It is a slow process, and multiplication takes time to reach the point of exponential growth.

+ **The pastor must be a model.** The pastor must lead the way by developing leaders and also by leading a group.

- **Identify your process.** Every community is different, and what works one place may not work in another setting. Learn through trial and error.

- **It is not a program but a process.** Be ready to change constantly.

# CHAPTER 15

# Excels in Teaching God's Word

## Ken Coley

EXCELLENCE IN TEACHING GOD'S WORD is a critical component when developing a Sunday school ministry that glorifies Christ, stimulates spiritual growth in believers, and ministers to both the members and the community that God has called them to serve. The apostle Paul said it best when he wrote and expressed his gratitude for the inspiring growth he saw in the saints at Thessalonica:

> For this reason we also thank God without ceasing, because when you received the word of God which you heard from us, you welcomed it not as the word of men, but as it is in truth, the word of God, which also effectively works in you who believe (1 Thess. 2:13, emphasis added).

The litmus test for excellence in teaching is the transformation of believers' lives by the power of the Holy Spirit, and one of the major sources of this change is the influence of God's Word on an individual's thinking, believing, and behaving. Where there is effective teaching, there is *change*—in knowledge, in perspective, in attitudes, and ultimately, in behavior. *Where there is no change, no teaching and learning has occurred.* Yes, there can be passive consent, or short-term memory of a set of facts. But long term, a lasting change in a person's life is necessary to say that teaching and learning has been successful and effective, and that God's word is "performing its work in you who believe."

With over thirty years of experience teaching Sunday school in three different locations, this writer has discovered that the key to seeing this change happen is the short, but powerful word, *engage*. Content that is taught with the use of techniques that offer the opportunity for Bible study participants to engage with God's word, with the instructor, and with his/her group is more likely to take hold in the believer's mind and heart than instructional approaches in which the participants remain passive. Students learn more when they actively engage with the content than when they sit, listen, take notes, and watch. How can your leaders be most effective in a form of teaching that engages the members in order to have a Sunday school or small group ministry that truly excels?

## THE CHALLENGE
A familiar story—

My wife and I were new in the community and set out to visit a variety of churches as we prayed about where the Lord wanted us to serve. The friendly greeter met us at the door of an average, small-town church and escorted us to a couples' class. After a few brief remarks and a time of prayer, the teacher began the lesson... by reading from the teacher's book. Unfortunately, the Bible study did not improve from there. The teacher read from the resource book the entire hour, interrupted only by the occasional pause to ask, "Does anyone have any questions or comments?"

This is truly tragic! But everyone knows that this scenario plays out all across the country every Sunday in groups and churches of all sizes. After working with hundreds of lay teachers as well as professional educators, it is this educator's observation that most Christians who are willing to teach a Sunday school class are well-meaning and sincere about presenting the gospel in a winsome way and wish to see fellow group members grow. Unfortunately, many do not know how to get better, and the leaders around them are struggling with just maintaining the status quo. Some barriers to change may include:

- We don't have enough teachers, so we can't risk losing the ones we have.

- If we wanted to establish effective teaching standards, we aren't sure what that looks like.

- We lack the expertise to provide the training that the teachers need.

- Apparently, the students approve of the teacher; they keep coming.

- This teacher has taught that class longer than I am old.... I don't dare challenge his approach.

These struggles and others hold discipleship leaders back from boldly stepping forward and saying, "Let's learn how to engage our members in meaningful ways so that God's Word comes to life in them!"

Richland Creek Community Church in Wake Forest, North Carolina had a modest beginning like so many church plants. The young pastor, along with some courageous believers, stepped out on faith and leased space in a local middle school, including the gym for worship and a handful of groups of all shapes and sizes. The gospel was clearly proclaimed, and neighborhood families began to join them in the ministry. Bible study on Sunday mornings was emphasized, but because of rapid growth and the absence of expectations or standards, that dimension of the church began to flounder. At the request of the pastor, the church called a part-time educational leader who began meeting with a cohort of enthusiastic, adult teachers. They agreed to pull together as a team to insure that the Sunday school ministry would become one of the strengths of the church. Over a period of ten years, the Sunday school participation more than quadrupled. How did they utilize a focus on teaching to lead the congregation to excel?

## KEYS TO EXCELLING

First, as a team of peers working together, the teachers *fashioned a philosophy of teaching Bible study* that began with focusing on Scripture and taught one book at a time. While other discipleship programs at Richland Creek Community Church provided instruction in the areas of relationships, finances, spiritual disciplines, parenting, evangelism, and other valuable topics, the Sunday school ministry was built entirely on the teaching of God's Word one book at a time. This was agreed upon and followed one hundred percent.

Second, *the teachers agreed to meet regularly and discuss not only the substance of the passages for the upcoming lessons, but also spend time discussing in detail how the lesson content would be presented.* Here's a brief outline that most teachers used while preparing his/her Bible study:

**Connection:** Begin with a "hook" that connects the participant's prior experience with the content.

**Context:** Select important aspects of the cultural, historical, or geographical setting of the study.

**Context in the book:** Clarify how the passage is tied to the overall flow/theme of the book.

**Content:** The major focus of that day's study—what is God saying to us in his Word?

**Comprehension:** Take time to measure the participant's understanding.

**Conviction:** What are aspects of my life about which the Lord is speaking to me?

**Challenge for application:** How might I think, feel, or respond differently this week based on this study?

The teachers' meeting includes *reflecting on how the various approaches worked* with their participants during specific, instructional episodes the previous week. Such reflection about the effectiveness of teaching strategies and the needs of participants is a vital aspect of a teacher improving his/her teaching skills.

Third, the Richland Creek Bible study teachers determined that it is vital to engage their members in the teaching/learning episode. This author has found that this is the greatest difference between growing Sunday school classes and those that are stagnant or declining. What happens during a study session that causes members to fall more deeply in love with God's Word? What will allow a group member to be prepared to study more effectively on his own in the future? *Engagement!*

## DIFFERENTIATION IN INSTRUCTIONAL TECHNIQUES

Effective teaching includes the awareness that students are not all alike. Teaching and learning is not a "one size fits all" experience. Most teachers lead their groups based on two pictures or models in their minds. First, a teacher will teach based on the methodologies of his/her favorite teacher. Second, a teacher will teach based on how he/she learns best. But not everyone in the room perceives and processes the material in the same way as the teacher. *It is the obligation of a Christlike teacher to adjust his/her teaching style to accommodate the variety of learners that God has brought into the room.* Here are just three of these potential differences:

- Visual learner: I learn best when you write on the board, show me a picture, or use an object to illustrate your point. If I see it, I will remember it.

- Auditory learner: I learn best by listening to an interesting lecture, by hearing other view points, and by having the opportunity to articulate my own understanding.

- Haptic, tactile, or kinesthetic learner: I love to move, touch, create with my hands, and in general, interact with the material in an active way. Sitting for long periods of time is a negative for me.

Note: The majority of adults learn best when visual representations are included and when they get to discuss and interact with other class members.

## ENGAGE THROUGH ACTIVE LEARNING TECHNIQUES (ALTs)

As previously stated, adult learners stay focused better when they are actively involved in the Bible study as opposed to listening passively to a lecture. And merely asking, "Does anyone have any questions?" does not count as discussion or participation. Teachers need to be challenged to plan intentionally to design participation opportunities in their Bible study preparation. This is not to say that any lecture is a poor second to active learning. What needs to take place is a balance between the teacher presenting the information that he/she has researched prior to class with episodes in which the group members interact with the teacher, the Scripture, and one another. A teacher who is new to this approach might set a goal of making use of two ALTs each lesson, placing new ones at different places in the presentation each week. Remember that ALTs occur when the group is making a response or participating in some active way as opposed to passively listening to the leader as they talk or present. As both the teacher and the group become accustomed to the new expectations, the number of ALTs per lesson could increase to three or four activities each week. And one more thing: An ALT can take as little time as it takes for group members to show their response after considering a question and giving it a "thumbs up" or a "thumbs down." Fifteen seconds!

## ACTIVE LEARNING TECHNIQUES

Consider the following examples of active learning techniques, along with suggestions of where each might work best. No one would do all of these in one teaching session, but this does demonstrate how activities can occur at different times in the lesson:

**Before the class begins:** The leader prepares five statements that connect with the theme or topic of the lesson. As each member enters, he/she is given one of the statements and asked to consider a brief response. As members arrive, they are encouraged to interact with members who have different statements. Each reads his or her statement to the other, and then shares his own reaction to the statement. (Technique: *Tea Party*)

**Review:** How many of you encountered a situation this week that reminded you of the application theme from last week's study? Raise your hand.... (Technique: *Polling*)

**Connect:** This week's study involves the concept of forgiveness. I want you to think about a time when you chose to forgive someone who had offended you. [Pause thirty seconds.] Now, I want you to turn to the person next to you, your shoulder partner, and briefly describe the decision that you made. [Pause sixty seconds.] Thanks for participating. Who will share what you and your partner discussed with the entire class? (Technique: *Think-Pair-Share*)

**Context:** These events influenced the culture and political environment in our passage today. I am going to put you into two teams, and I would like for you to place these events in chronological order, beginning with the one that occurred first. The team that finishes first gets first run at the box of doughnuts that I brought for snack today! (Technique: *Get It Straight*)

**Content:** Please take a look at the first five verses in our passage today, and while you read them, I want you to look for the identity and description of the group that Jesus is addressing. Begin reading. [Pause for one minute.] When you have made the identification, please look up so I will know that you are ready to answer. Who can help us identify the characters? [Discuss.] Now that we know who the players are, please continue reading and look for information about how they responded to Jesus' teachings. Please look up when you have completed the entire passage and have an answer. (Technique: *Read with a Purpose*)

**Check for comprehension:** I placed three cards in your seat. I am going to ask you two important questions about today's topic, and for each question I would like for you to hold up one of the cards that indicates your level of understanding—*red* means, "Stop. I am not ready to move on"; *yellow* means, "I'm not sure. I need to examine this some more"; *green* means, "I got the concept, and I'm ready to move on." (Technique: *Stoplight: checking for levels of understanding*)

**Confirm conviction:** Using a note card, I would like for you to reflect on the most important issue confronting your life this week in regard to this study. I would like you to write a statement about what you think the Holy Spirit is asking you to change and how you plan to respond. This will be between you and the Lord, and I will not call on you or ask to read your card. (Technique: *Writing for Understanding*)

**Challenge for application:** This week the Lord wants to impact people around you. Using one of the sticky notes, write down what you can do this week as a response to today's study. After you have written on one or more notes, I want you to come up and place your note under one of the four categories I have written on the whiteboard: home, community, work, the mall (Technique: *Post-It Note Response*)

## MOVING FORWARD IN PURSUIT OF EXCELLENCE

- Gather a group of teachers together—as many as are willing to participate. Begin a serious dialogue about how teachers influence their members to fall more in love with God's Word and make it a real and vibrant part of their lives. This discussion should include an awareness of the *differences within the class*—backgrounds, biblical knowledge, personalities, and learning styles. From this discussion, the group fashions a philosophy about Sunday school teaching and learning.

- Work together to select a suitable curriculum resource that will support a commitment to *study God's Word in a systematic way.*

- Initiate a discussion on *active learning techniques* and find ways to share Bible study teaching plans and tips about successful teaching episodes with each other. Many teachers would profit from getting together weekly or monthly to reflect on effective ways to involve adults in the teaching/learning process. Some teachers would likewise enjoy using social media for immediate sharing of ideas.

And remember the goal. Your teachers will say about their group members: *You accepted it not as the word of men, but for what it really is, the word of God, which also performs its work in you who believe.*

# CHAPTER 16

# A Tour of Some Sunday Schools That Excel

## Steve R. Parr

OUR JOURNEY HAS TAKEN US across North America. In the course of fifteen chapters, we have heard testimony of Sunday schools that excel in Canada, Alabama, Arkansas, California, Delaware, Florida, Georgia, Indiana, Louisiana, Maryland, New Hampshire, New Mexico, New York, North Carolina, Ohio, Oklahoma, Texas, Virginia, and West Virginia. The chapter that follows will pull all of the key principles together, providing you with a template to lead your Sunday school ministry to excel. Before we make the turn, we want to take a brief glimpse of five more Sunday schools that excel in Alabama, Mississippi, Texas, and two from North Carolina.

## LINDSEY LANE BAPTIST CHURCH IN ATHENS, ALABAMA

Lindsay Lane Baptist Church in Athens, Alabama has a Sunday school that excels by involving people in carrying out the vision of making disciples that worship, grow, and serve. This takes place mainly in the adult Sunday school through care groups. By having a care group time during Sunday school where the class meets in smaller groups, we are able to build relationships and develop leaders. Building relationships is the key to people staying, and developing leaders is the key to growing our Sunday school. By developing spiritually healthy leaders, we have a spiritually healthy Sunday school and church.

*Submitted by Sonny Schofield, Minister of Education*

## FIRST BAPTIST CHURCH OF SUMMIT, MISSISSIPPI

First Baptist Church Summit has a Sunday School that excels:

- by increasing in attendance from 383 in 2005 to 624 in 2011

- by using every Wednesday night midweek time for Sunday school classes to group together for prayer, fellowship, and sharing ministry and outreach assignments

- by having a pastor and minister of education in complete sync with the priority and utilization of Sunday school—these guys are an excellent model

- by penetrating their community with mission-minded campaigns worked through their Sunday school groups

- by being the intentional medium for church growth and community impact

*Submitted by Tom Crocker, Consultant at*
*LifeWay Christian Resources*

## LAWNDALE BAPTIST CHURCH IN GREENSBORO, NORTH CAROLINA

Lawndale Baptist Church has a Sunday school (Life Journey Groups), that excels because of their commitment to move people into a Life Journey Group and their commitment to start new groups. Each year Rodney Navey, along with the other staff, seek to enlarge the organization by adding new groups. They faced some difficult years with the discovery of structural flaws in the new worship center and soon to follow in their Family Life Center/Childhood Building. Through it all, they shuffled classes and maintained strong attendance. Presently challenged by space, Rodney is adding off campus Life Journey Groups to continue the value of starting new classes. It has its challenges, but they realize the health, growth, and outreach of the church rests in finding the gaps, training up leaders, and adding new Life Journey Groups. The staff also values the strength and consistency of a Bible study curriculum that guides each age group.

*Submitted by Keith Feather, Transformational Church*
*Consultant at LifeWay Christian Resources*

## FIRST BAPTIST CHURCH OF INDIAN TRAIL, NORTH CAROLINA

First Baptist Church of Indian Trail has a Sunday school that excels by having a pastor that knows the value of Sunday school and is immersed in its strategy. John Sprinkle organizes the education team, making sure each age level staff prioritizes the Life Group ministry especially when choosing leaders. John provides regular training for his adult leaders, provides a Life Group Manual, and consistently drives the purpose and expectations of Sunday school. He monitors and values the consistency of a Bible teaching curriculum while also allowing seasonal flexibility. For many years, this church and staff has mentored other churches in the Carolinas and across the US as Sunday School Missionaries. As they expand into multiple campuses, Sunday school remains a foundational strategy.

*Submitted by Keith Feather, Transformational Church Consultant at Lifeway Christian Resources*

## FIRST BAPTIST CHURCH OF FRISCO, TEXAS

This church has seen an amazing turnaround. In 2011 they grew by thirty-eight percent. Their growth is being accomplished through basic Sunday school principles. The church was not growing until the leaders caught the vision and began applying the principles that can make Sunday schools thrive.

*Submitted by Larry Golden, Consultant with Lifeway Christian Resources*

The final church testimony was brief but introduced a thought that begs the question, "What causes a Sunday school to thrive?" The final chapter answers that question, as the tour concludes with a plan to "excel-erate" your Sunday school.

# CHAPTER 17

# A Plan to Excel-erate Your Sunday School

## Steve R. Parr

OUR JOURNEY BEGAN WITH AFFIRMATIONS from Allan Taylor and David Francis as they introduced you to the authors and topics for this work. We then took a trip to Nashville, Tennessee and invited you to listen in as Dr. Thom Rainer and I discussed the state of Sunday school in today's culture. We left Nashville and have traveled across North America, observing actual churches that have excelled in leading a vibrant Sunday school ministry in a variety of settings, situations, and in spite of various challenges. Your Sunday school can excel. If they can do it, then you can do it. But, it will not be easy. Leading your Sunday school to excel requires purposeful leadership, patience, and the power of God.

Let's bring the journey to a conclusion by considering the best practices for a Sunday school that seeks to excel. How can you *Excel-erate* your Sunday school ministry? To accelerate is to cause an object to move forward. Since the theme of our journey is to *excel* we will graft the words excel and accelerate together and discover the keys to *EXCEL-ERATE* your Sunday school ministry. You will recognize these from the various case studies of the previous chapters and may use this to equip and communicate to leaders in your congregation to encourage them to excel-erate your ministry.

## E—ELEVATE THE STRATEGY

It is not possible to build anything of value up by talking it down. Some Sunday schools struggle because key leaders mock, criticize, or dismiss the strategy as irrelevant. Why would anyone possess any enthusiasm for a strategy that the pastor or staff devalues through their critiques? You must look past the words "Sunday school" and beyond any existing tradition, and analyze the potential of the principles if and when properly applied. Can subdividing your congregation into groups by life stage through which they gather regularly to develop relationships, pray for one another, minister to one another, engage in age-appropriate interactive Bible study, and work in concert to engage in missions and ministry to the unchurched potentially strengthen your church? Could such a strategy enhance the worship, provide more avenues for ministry to the congregation and the community, and serve as a venue to develop leaders? The answer is "yes," if it is given appropriate leadership and elevation.

Some pastors and leaders inadvertently devalue Sunday school by their silence. They do not criticize nor do they object. However, they may suppose that the strategy can thrive on autopilot. Enlisting teachers, assigning groups and rooms in which to meet, ordering the curriculum, and then standing back assuming the task is complete is a recipe for a failing Sunday school. Many Sunday school ministries are floundering because the pastor or key leaders have delegated administration to volunteers, who though well-meaning do not possess the knowledge or skills that lead the ministry to excel.

How about in your church? Is Sunday school one of the key priorities? If it is not, then you will be hard-pressed to have a

Sunday school that excels. A church can have more than one priority. On the other hand, if you have a dozen priorities you might as well have none. Vibrant churches usually have three to five key priorities and Sunday school or their small group strategy is clearly communicated as one of them. Can you have six or seven priorities? You can, but the others become more and more diluted and ultimately devalued. Your Sunday school ministry must be elevated as one of the churches priorities through the pastor's preaching, pastor's verbal affirmation, the affirmation of the staff in larger congregations, through written communication, through calendaring, and through commitment as a key priority. How can your church do a better job of elevating the strategy of Sunday school?

## X—EXPRESS APPRECIATION

The ministry of Sunday school cannot excel without the involvement of a good number of volunteers. Pastors and staff members play a critical role, but the strategy cannot possibly be implemented without lay men and women exercising their gifts and offering their personal commitment. Volunteers by definition do not expect to be paid for their services. However, that does not mean that they have no need of some form of reward and recognition. While it is true that their rewards are in heaven, it is also true that acknowledgement along the way can make the journey much more pleasant.

The wages that work best in compensating volunteers are expressions of appreciation and the good news is that all leaders have the currency to make the payment. How and how often are you expressing appreciation to those who volunteer their time in leading the Sunday school? You must remember that the Sunday school strategy is high maintenance but fortunately high in return for the investment also. The commitment to prepare and teach week after week with the additional responsibilities of leading in outreach, ministry, and fellowship can be draining physically and emotionally. You must remember that most Sunday school leaders also have additional responsibilities in your church as well as in their families, places of employment, and communities.

Three quick ways that you can energize your leaders and give them the fuel that prevents burnout and turnover in your volunteer leaders. First, frequently express appreciation by making phone calls, sending texts or messages through electronic and social networks, and sending letters of appreciation. You must personalize these and not send in mass for greatest effect. Secondly, give public affirmation to leaders from the pulpit and the platform on several occasions throughout the year. Provide the recognition for all leaders, but also for select leaders when achievements are made such as launching new groups or releasing leaders. For example, have all leaders who participated in the past weekend's training time stand so that the congregation can express appreciation. You are also providing a subtle message for those who did not participate. Thirdly, provide tangible awards when and if possible based on available resources in your church. Gift certificates, special meals, discounts, and awards are not expected from volunteers but can be very affirming.

## C—COMMUNICATE THE CORRECT PURPOSE

Many Sunday school ministries and leaders struggle with gaining any momentum because they misunderstand, miscommunicate, or fail to communicate the correct purpose of the ministry. The purpose as perceived by the members will affect attitudes, quality, and participation. A vast majority of church members and leaders will tell you that the purpose of Sunday school is to "study the Bible" or something along those lines. If that were true, then every Sunday school would excel.

Sunday school is centered on Bible study and must be built on the study of God's Word. However, if that is the purpose then the leader can show up late since the Bible study does not start until twenty minutes or so into the session. Others will opt to go to worship only because the pastor will provide a study of Scripture at the core of his sermon. Outreach will struggle because it is not necessary in and of itself to study the Bible. Guests will be lacking because they are not necessary for members to study the Bible. To suppose that the reason for Sunday school is to study the Bible is not incorrect but is incomplete.

The purpose of Sunday school is to engage the congregation in the fulfillment of the Great Commission. Your purpose statement may be more eloquent but should be based on this premise given that the instructions are from Jesus himself. We are to "teach them to obey" but the Great Commission goes further. The Sunday school will excel when the lost are being reached out to, lives are being changed, and leaders are being released. That allows for ministry to the members and outreach to the community. Be sure to communicate the purpose clearly and correctly.

## E—EQUIP YOUR LEADERS

Research shows that the number one determining factor in whether a Sunday school excels is the frequency of the training. The data is highlighted in *Sunday School That Really Works,* and in summary shows that churches that train leaders tend to be growing and those who fail to provide equipping tend to be declining. Why is that? We know that only God can bring growth and that the Holy Spirit is the key driver. However, God works through the body of Christ, the church.

How do members know the purpose unless it is communicated? As you consider each of the dynamics of Sunday schools that really excel, you must ask where and how the leaders will discover how to implement them. It will not happen by osmosis, or all leaders would excel in leading Sunday schools across the nation. You can have good-hearted, well-meaning leaders and volunteers who love the Lord and yet fail to lead the Sunday school to excel. The reason is because they lack the skills to do so. Spiritual growth comes as believers spend time in God's Word, in prayer, and in worship.

How do leaders grow in their skills? They must be equipped. You can be creative with schedules and those vary church to church. However, Sunday schools that excel design systematic ways to encourage the spiritual growth as well as the skills of leaders throughout the year. Doesn't it make sense that "skilled leaders" who love the Lord will have better results than "unskilled leaders" who love the Lord? Take initiative in equipping your leaders through reading, gatherings, seminars, conferences, web sources, and purposeful time with volunteers. Otherwise the results will be random instead of excellent.

## L—LEAD YOUR GROUPS TO MINISTER TOGETHER

"Soon afterward He [Jesus] was traveling from one town and village to another, preaching and telling the good news of the kingdom of God. The Twelve were with Him" (Luke 8:1 HCSB). Jesus was purposeful in getting his group into the community. Sunday schools begin to excel when the focus turns outward as well as inward. The groups must learn to minister together in at least two ways. The most common and most obvious is ministry to the members. Meeting the needs of those who attend regularly tends to happen with minimal effort. The first challenge is to help the groups minister to those who are members, yet attend sporadically or perhaps never attend at all. The Sunday school class is the most obvious source for ministry to members because they have a list (a roll) and by virtue of taking attendance have direct awareness of attendance patterns. Asking groups to focus on ministry contacts and reporting the total number each week is one way to make this emphasis. The key is to equip every group to minister to every member by maintaining regular ministry contact without regard to frequency of attendance. Actually, the greatest need many be of those who attend less frequently.

Take groups to the next level by emphasizing ministry outside of the class. Challenge classes to conduct community ministry projects several times each year. Hurting people are found in every community. As you identify and seek to meet those needs you simultaneously enhance the connection of the groups, meet needs of hurting community members, and open up doors of outreach by loving on community members in Jesus's name. The potential effect of the reputation of your church in the community can be exponentially increased by every class that commits to take their group to do ministry in the community as Jesus modeled with the apostles.

## E—EXPAND THE ENROLLMENT

Help your leaders grasp the following principle: *The more people your group ministers to during the week, the more people that will attend the Bible study on Sunday* (or whenever your group meets). What does that have to do with "enrollment?" You cannot expect the attendance to increase by ministering to fewer people. For example, suppose one class has ten on their roll that they minister to regularly. Suppose another class has forty on their roll they minister to regularly. If only half of those ministered to attend in the second group, they will have twenty present, whereas the first group will only have ten if everyone shows up.

Every leader desires for every member to be present every week. But, that will not likely happen for very practical reasons. Every Sunday, churches have members who are out of town, those who are sick, those who have physical limitations, some who have to work, and any other variety of reasons that are not spiritual in nature. In addition, there are members who are not as committed. The tendency is to remove those from the class membership if they rarely or never attend. However, as stated earlier, you cannot increase attendance by ministering to fewer people.

Every group and every church should be purposeful in seeking to expand the enrollment. If you minister to everyone you will typically have forty to sixty percent present for your Bible study. Keep in mind that a person need not be a member of the church to be a member of the group. Identify, invite, enroll, and minister to as many people as possible. Pray for each one regularly, invite members and prospects to several fellowships, maintain regular contacts, and minister as needs are discovered. You will find that the larger the enrollment, the greater the attendance if you follow through on the ministry aspect. Remove members at the point you can no longer minister. Failing to attend is not a signal to remove them but rather to reach out and minister during their time of need.

## R—REACH OUT TO THE UNCHURCHED

Sunday schools that excel are committed to reach out to the community as well as ministering to the congregation. Every church and class has hurting people that the group should be attentive to. However, no difficulty that any member is facing is as severe as the condition of a person who does not know Jesus Christ as Savior and Lord. Ministering to the members is easier because they are in your presence each and every week. Reaching out to the unchurched requires intentionality.

The unchurched consist of believers and unbelievers in that the groups should be reaching out to any and all that are not actively committed to worship and Bible study. Believers and unbelievers alike have ministry needs that need attention. However, the unchurched unbeliever also needs to hear the gospel. Unchurched believers need to be encouraged to grow in their faith and that is not possible apart from worship and the word of God.

Sunday school classes are uniquely positioned to reach out to the unchurched because they tend to be organized by life stage. Children can reach out to children, students to students, college age young adults to college age young adults, young married adults to other young married adults, parents of college students to parents of college students, and senior adults to senior adults. These represent examples, and larger churches are subdivided into even more life stages.

Can a college student reach a senior adult? Certainly, but that would not typically happen. Take high-school students as an example. They are living experts on the culture of what it means to be a high-school student at this point and time. Who would be better equipped to reach high-school students? The challenge is to lead your groups to engage in outreach as well as Bible study and fellowship, understanding that evangelism and outreach are essential for a Sunday school to excel.

## A—ASSIGN GROUPS BY LIFE STAGE

Organizing groups according to life stage is obvious in younger age groups. Although you can place all preschoolers in one group, it is better to have bed babies and kindergarten children in separate classes. Dividing the preschool into at least two classes if possible is advantageous in regard to the ministry and learning activities that you can provide. Likewise, you can put first through sixth grade together in your children's ministry, but obviously the six- and eleven-year-old children are worlds apart in terms of maturity. The ideal is to have a class for each year (first grade, second grade, etc.), but the degree to which you can do that is based on the attendance and resources available.

Middle-school and high-school students are affected, though to a lesser degree. An eighteen-year-old girl may have difficulty relating to a twelve-year-old boy. All of the students can be placed in one group, but there is an advantage to have a middle-school and a high-school group that meets separately. Rarely will a person disagree with the wisdom of subdividing the younger groups to some degree to maximize the learning environment.

What about with the adult ministry? Some members propose that the best strategy is to let everyone go where he or she is most comfortable. The problem is... what is comfortable to the regular attendees may not be as comfortable to the guests. Suppose a young couple at twenty-four years of age visits a church. When they attend a small group like Sunday school, what are they looking for? Bible study? Yes, but honestly they are looking to connect with other young couples.

You need a group that consists of young couples. Why is that? Guests connect best, and are more likely to assimilate or join your congregation, if they quickly establish relationships. Can they do that with a couple in their fifties? In theory they can, but it is not likely. Organizing adults as well as younger groups by ages or life stages will provide the best system through which outreach and assimilation are enhanced, as well as attention to unique learning dynamics for various generations.

## T—TEACH AGE-APPROPRIATE APPLICABLE BIBLE STUDIES

Teaching is the most obvious component of Sunday school and small group ministries. However, leaders should not assume that the teaching will automatically be effective. Training is essential to encourage and equip your leaders to provide Bible study experiences that are appropriate to their unique audiences. The manner in which three-year-olds are instructed will obviously differ from the methods applied to the college-age students. Sunday school leaders must learn to specialize by becoming students themselves of the age group to which they are assigned.

What is unique about the life stage of the group the teacher leads? How do they learn best at this stage of their growth? What are their attention spans like? How can the learners participate? Untrained leaders left to their own devices, will be forced to revert to their own learning experiences which may or may not have been healthy. Consider how you can assist leaders through training opportunities to become experts in leading their designated audience. Bringing in someone with expertise, taking leaders to a specialized conference, or providing books and resources that focus on preschool, children, students, or adults is well advised. Also bear in mind that the needs of young adults will vary considerably from senior adults. Do not assume that all adults fall into the same category when it comes to equipping leaders to understand and best communicate in the most appropriate way with their group.

### E- EXPAND THE LEADERSHIP BASE

Focus on growing your leaders, and they will grow your congregation. The key is to inspire them in their personal development, emphasizing growth spiritually as well as growth in skills. Growing in skills is important because it will result in a leader who knows how to develop other leaders. Take an individual class or group as an example. Suppose one teacher provides all of the leadership except for one class secretary who keeps records. Suppose another teacher enlists six members to serve in various roles and works with them regularly to carry out their responsibilities. Which group is most likely to be effective? Will it be the group with one key leader or the group with seven leaders serving? Expand the leadership base by enlisting and equipping as many leaders as possible. Equip all teachers to do likewise, and the attendance will increase as the leadership base increases.

The number of groups will also need to increase as the leadership base grows. No church has ever sustained growth without increasing the number of groups. Suppose a church has ten groups or classes that average about one hundred in attendance. They will not likely grow to 150 with the existing groups. Four or five new groups will have to be created. Expand the base of your Sunday school by creating new groups. The groups that have the most difficulty doing this are those in the adult ministry. Sunday schools that excel motivate and equip leaders of adult classes and groups to embrace the creation of new classes. New groups reach people that existing groups will not reach. Equip your leaders to create new groups by emphasizing that the health of a group is not measured solely by attendance, but by the number of leaders that are developed and released during the course of the year. The groups that grasp this principle are the ones that lead the Sunday school to excel.

**Other books on Sunday school
by Steve R. Parr**

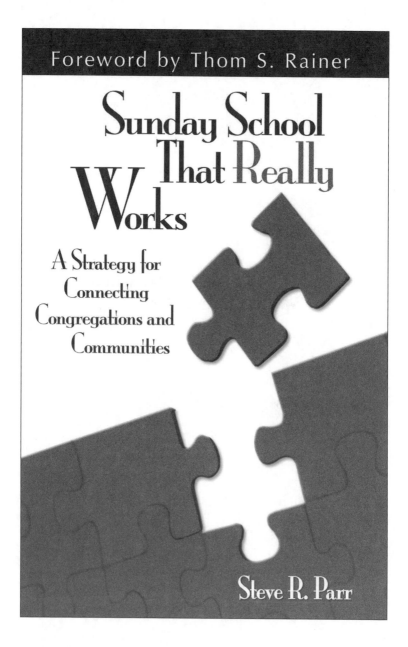

Foreword by Thom S. Rainer

# Sunday School That Really Works

## A Strategy for Connecting Congregations and Communities

Steve R. Parr

ISBN 978-0-8254-3567-6

# Sunday School That Really Responds

## Wisdom for Confronting 24 Common Sunday School Emergencies

Steve R. Parr

ISBN 978-0-8254-4064-9